Lecture Notes in Computer Science 9391

Commenced Publication in 1973
Founding and Former Series Editors:
Gerhard Goos, Juris Hartmanis, and Jan van Leeuwen

More information about this series at http://www.springer.com/series/7409

Xiaokui Xiao · Zhenjie Zhang (Eds.)

Web-Age Information Management

WAIM 2015 International Workshops: HENA, HRSUNE
Qingdao, China, June 8–10, 2015
Revised Selected Papers

 Springer

Editors
Xiaokui Xiao
School of Computer Engineering
Nanyang Technological University
Singapore
Singapore

Zhenjie Zhang
Advanced Digital Sciences Center
Singapore
Singapore

ISSN 0302-9743   ISSN 1611-3349 (electronic)
Lecture Notes in Computer Science
ISBN 978-3-319-23530-1   ISBN 978-3-319-23531-8   (eBook)
DOI 10.1007/978-3-319-23531-8

Library of Congress Control Number: 2015942482

LNCS Sublibrary: SL3 – Information Systems and Applications, incl. Internet/Web, and HCI

Springer Cham Heidelberg New York Dordrecht London

Printed on acid-free paper

Springer International Publishing AG Switzerland is part of Springer Science+Business Media
(www.springer.com)

Preface

The International Conference on Web-Age Information Management (WAIM) is a leading venue for researchers, practitioners, developers, and users to share and exchange ideas, results, experiences, techniques, and tools in connection with all aspects of Web data management. As the 16th event in the increasingly popular series, WAIM 2015 was held in Qingdao, China, during June 8–10, 2015, and it attracted participants from all over the world.

Along with the main conference, the WAIM workshops also provide an international forum for researchers to discuss research results. There were two workshops held in conjunction with WAIM 2015:

- International Workshop on Heterogeneous Information Network Analysis and Applications (HENA 2015)
- 2nd International Workshop on Human Aspects of Making Recommendations in and for Social Ubiquitous Networking Environments (HRSUNE 2015)

Both workshops were selected after a public call-for-proposals process, and each of them focuses on a specific area that contributes to the main themes of WAIM. In total, 9 papers were accepted into the workshops. We would like to thank the workshop organizers and Program Committee members for their tremendous effort in making the WAIM 2015 workshops a success. In addition, we are grateful to the main conference organizers for their generous support.

July 2015

Xiaokui Xiao
Zhenjie Zhang

Organization

HENA 2015

Workshop Chairs

Bin Wu	Beijing University of Posts and Telecommunications, China
Bin Zhou	National University of Defense Technology, China
Chuan Shi	Beijing University of Posts and Telecommunications, China
Philip S. Yu	University of Illinois at Chicago, USA

Program Committee

Yueguo Chen	Renmin University of China, China
Jiuming Huang	National University of Defense Technology, China
Qing He	Institute of Computing Technology, Chinese Academy of Sciences, China
Liang Liu	Beijing University of Posts and Telecommunications, China
Shenghua Liu	Institute of Computing Technology, Chinese Academy of Sciences, China
Youfang Lin	Beijing Jiaotong University, China
Xiangnan Kong	Worcester Polytechnic Institute, USA
Zhaohui Peng	Shandong University, China
Huawei Shen	Institute of Computing Technology, Chinese Academy of Sciences, China
Jie Tang	Tsinghua University, China
Zhi Wei	New Jersey Institute of Technology, USA
Yanghua Xiao	Fudan University, China
Yun Xiong	Fudan University, China
Zhenyu Yan	Adobe Systems Inc., USA
Ning Yang	Sichuan University, China
Lei Zou	Peking University, China

HRSUNE 2015

Workshop Chairs

Tiffany Tang	Kean University, USA
Olga C. Santos	aDeNu Research group, UNED, Spain

Program Committee

Mária Bieliková	Slovak University of Technology, Slovakia
Jesus G. Boticario	aDeNu Research Group, UNED, Spain
Iván Cantador	Universidad Autónoma de Madrid, Spain
Keith C. Chan	Hong Kong Polytechnic University, HK SAR
Evandro Costa	Federal University of Alagoas, Brazil
Alexander Felfernig	Graz University of Technology, Austria
Marco de Gemmis	University of Bari, Italy
Dietmar Jannach	TU Dortmund, Germany
Milos Kravcik	RWTH Aachen University, Germany
Pasquale Lops	University of Bari "Aldo Moro", Italy
Estefanía Martín	Universidad Rey Juan Carlos, Spain
Marko Tkalčič	Johannes Kepler University, Austria
Katrien Verbert	Vrije Universiteit Brussel, Belgium
Robert Walker	University of Calgary, Canada
Pinata Winoto	Kean University, USA

Contents

HENA 2015

A Distributed RDF Storage
and Query Model Based on HBase

Keran Li[✉], Bin Wu, and Bai Wang

Beijing Key Laboratory of Intelligent Telecommunications Software
and Multimedia, Beijing University of Posts and Telecommunications,
Beijing 100876, China
likerann@gmail.com, {wubin,wangbai}@bupt.edu.cn

Abstract. Now we are living in an interconnected world and the amount of heterogeneous information data such as RDF is continually increasing. A lot has been done to find the solution to manage huge amount of RDF data. The solutions based on RDBMS have significant scalability issues considering the magnitude of data in modern time. In this paper we describe our solution to store and query RDF data in the cloud based on HBase and MapReduce. A vertical-partitioning-like model is used in HBase to reduce the table size and to obtain a good performance of SPARQL query. For complex query on large data, we propose to use cascading MapReduce job on HBase to enhance efficiency. Our experiments on LUBM show that our system can store large RDF graphs and can obtain good query efficiency.

Keywords: RDF · Heterogeneous · Hbase · Vertical partition · Mapreduce

1 Introduction

The Resource Description Framework is a way to describe and model information, typically of the World Wide Web. RDF data is essentially heterogeneous information data. As RDF is meant to be a standard for describing the Web resources, a large and ever expanding set of data and it has strong real-timeness [1], methods [2, 3, 5] must be devised to store and retrieve such a large data set. To store and query RDF data, many systems have been built, firstly within the Semantic Web community such as Jena[1] and Sesame [18]. RDF storage, indexing and query processing have also attracted interest from the data management community. And lately, commercial database management systems also started providing support for RDF, such as Oracle 11 g [19] or IBM DB2 10.1 [20].

While very efficient, most existing RDF stores rely on a centralized approach, with one server running very specialized hardware. RDF data are not structured data and RDF graph can be very large, which makes management difficult for conventional solutions. With the tremendous increase in data size, such solutions will likely not be able to scale up. Recently, more and more researchers have focused on distributed RDF data management.

---

[1] Apache Jena, http://jena.apache.org.

© Springer International Publishing Switzerland 2015
X. Xiao and Z. Zhang (Eds.): WAIM 2015, LNCS 9391, pp. 3–15, 2015.
DOI: 10.1007/978-3-319-23531-8_1

In this paper, we introduced a solution of RDF storage and query in a distributed database: HBase. We design a new model in HBase to store RDF data. HBase is suitable to store unstructured or semi-structured data such as RDF and can support fast query. We design a vertical-partitioning-like model based on HBase to obtain less space occupation and more efficient query. MapReduce framework is used to efficiently ingest data into our system. To deal with complex query, we propose *path index* based on HBase. In complex queries, complex joins are always needed for RDF storage systems in the cloud. Path index is used to reduce the numbers of join operation, making it more efficient for complex query. We propose different means of querying in our system. For simple queries, we get the result by looking up some particular tables and path index using HBase API. For complex queries, we get the results with the help of cascading MapReduce. Moreover, our model also supports range queries and regular expression filter.

The remainder of this paper is organized as follows: in Sect. 2, we summarize the basics of RDF and HBase and introduce the related work of RDF management system. In Sect. 3, we describe our storage model for RDF. In Sect. 4, we introduce path index of RDF data based on HBase and MapReduce. In Sect. 5, we describe different means of querying based on our system. In Sect. 6, we present the results of our experiments. Finally, we conclude in Sect. 7.

2   Related Work

The Resource Description Framework (RDF)[2] is a family of World Wide Web Consortium (W3C) specifications originally designed as a metadata data model. It has come to be used as a general method for conceptual description or modeling of information that is implemented in web resources. The RDF data model is based upon the idea of making statements about resources (in particular web resources) in the form of *subject–predicate–object* expressions. Figure 1 shows an example of RDF data about information of teachers in universities using RDF graph.

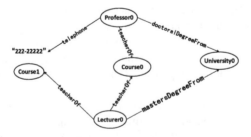

Fig. 1. RDF graph.

---

[2] RDF Current Status, http://www.w3.org/standards/techs/rdf#w3c_all.

For what concerns RDF querying, SPARQL[3] is the W3C standard for querying RDF graphs. SPARQL is not only a query language but also a kind of protocol. However, SPARQL can only be used to describe the query, not to execute the query.

Apache HBase is an open-source, distributed, versioned, non-relational database modeled after Google's Bigtable. Apache HBase provides Bigtable-like capabilities on top of Hadoop and HDFS. The data model of HBase corresponds to a sparse multi-dimensional sorted map with the following access pattern:

(Table, RowKey, Family, Column, Timestamp) $\rightarrow$ Value

Data is stored in tables that are structurally different from tables in relational databases. The rows of a table are sorted according to their *row key* and each row can have an arbitrary number of *columns*. However, in contrast to relational tables, two distinct rows of an HBase table do not have to have the same columns. Columns are grouped into *column families*.

In the next part, we'll look back on related work about RDF storage model both in RDBMS and in the cloud.

2.1 RDF Storage in RDBMS

Triple Store. This is the most simple and intuitive method for storing RDF data. All data are stored in exactly one table which consists of three columns: *subject*, *predicate* and *object*. Triple store is easy to implement. However, there are too many self-joins when querying the table and therefore lead to a bad performance.

Horizontal Store. This method puts all data about a particular subject into one corresponding row. The advantage of horizontal store is that it's easy to design and fast to query on a single subject because all information about the subject is in just one row. But there can be too many columns to store and may lead to too many empty values. Finally, in many cases, a subject may have more than one object under some predicates, which cannot be satisfied in RDBMS.

Property Table Store. Researchers developing the Jena Semantic Web toolkit, Jena2 [6, 7] proposed the use of property tables to speed up queries over triple-stores. They proposed two types of property tables. The first type, which we call a *clustered property table*, contains clusters of properties that tend to be defined together. Multiple property tables with different clusters of properties may be created.

The second type of property table, termed a *property-class table*, exploits the type property of subjects to cluster similar sets of subjects together in the same table. A property may exist in multiple property-class tables.

Vertical Partitioning. Abadi et al. [4, 8] proposed storage of RDF data using a fully decomposed storage model (DSM). The triples are rewritten into n two-column tables where n is the number of unique properties in the data. *Vertical Partitioning* model

---

doesn't store empty values and can store multi-values. Based on the idea of vertical partitioning, we design a similar model in HBase, and make some changes to enhance the efficiency, which will be demonstrated in the following sections.

2.2   RDF Storage in the Cloud

In [9], the authors surveyed large-scale RDF data management architectures and systems designed for a cloud environment and made a lot of comparisons and evaluations on various kinds of RDF data management solutions in the cloud.

Another study [10] presented methods for processing RDF data directly on Hadoop with MapReduce. Files on Hadoop now cannot be modified randomly which may limit many features such as update operation for RDF applications. Recent studies [11, 12] based on Hadoop use data index to improve the efficiency of data access, but these studies are not mature enough to be adopted by the community.

A study [13] presented a system for large-scale RDF data based on HBase. But it doesn't provide detailed explanation about its storage schema. Some studies [14, 21] use a six indexes structure for storing RDF triples. The six indexes (PSO, POS, SPO, SOP, OPS and OSP) cover all possible combination of RDF triples. Authors of [15] proposed to store RDF triples in three HBase tables (Ts, Tp and To) which take subject, predicate and object as row key respectively and use HBase API to query.

Roshan et al. proposed *Rya* [17] to manage RDF data based on Accumulo[4], which is similar to HBase. Rya uses three tables (SPO, POS, and OSP) to store RDF data. These tables store the triples in the Accumulo Row ID and order the subject, predicate and object differently for each table. This solution utilizes the row-sorting scheme of Accumulo to efficiently store and query triples across multiple Accumulo tablets. Rya supports large data and can get results fast for most queries. However, Rya is not efficient for complex query for time-consuming indexed nested loops join.

With the increase in data size, centralized approach will not likely able to meet the demands while distributed solutions are still developing. To find a better solution, in this paper we propose a new model based on HBase. In the next section, the model will be discussed.

3   RDF Storage Model

Our storage schema is different from most existing distributed solutions such as Rya. We propose the RDF storage model in HBase based on vertical partitioning. We create two tables (*Pso, Pos*) for each predicate. Assume the number of unique predicate is p, there will be $2p$ HBase tables in our model. In each of these Pso tables, the predicate is stored only once as the table name, the subjects that define that predicate as row key and the object values for those subjects as columns. There will be only one column family in each table. Table Pos is just the same with Pso, except that the subject needs to switch place with the object. The two-table solution creates index for both subjects

---

[4] Accumulo, http://accumulo.apache.org/.

Table 1. HBase tables for predicate "teacherOf".

SO		OS	
Row Key	**ColumnFamily: cf**	**Row Key**	**ColumnFamily: cf**
Lecturer0	cf: Course0	**Course0**	cf: Lecturer0
	cf: Course1		cf: Lecturer2
Lecturer1	cf: Course1	**Course1**	cf: Lecturer0
	cf: Course3		cf: Lecturer1
Lecturer2	cf: Course0	**Course2**	cf: Lecturer2
	cf: Course2	**Course3**	cf: Lecturer1
	cf: Course3		cf: Lecturer2

and objects and thus improves the efficiency. The two tables for predicate "teacherOf" can be presented by Table 1.

Compared to Rya, this model takes less space. Each triple in Rya is stored three times, while in our model we don't need to store predicate and each triple (except predicate) is stored only twice. Rya takes Accumulo as backend. Accumulo is very similar to HBase, both of which are open source implementation of Google Bigtable. To compare the two models in space occupation, we use HBase as the backend of Rya in Sect. 6. The result shows that the space taken of Rya is more than twice as much as our model.

The advantages of our model in HBase are as follows (compared to models in RDBMS and other models in the cloud):

Great Reliability. As a distributed, scalable, big data store, our model in HBase can store very large RDF data. More importantly, because there is no single point of failure in HBase (There are more than one master node in HBase) and HBase is architected on HDFS, our solution can guarantee great reliability.

Space Saving. Compared to most models in RDBMS, our model does not store empty values. What' more, as mentioned before, our model does not store predicate, thus saving a lot of space compared to other models in the cloud.

Fast Query. We create B+ tree like index for both subjects and objects by creating two tables for each predicate, making it efficient to query on a particular subject or object. The row key is indexed and sorted, making table join relatively efficient and range queries possible.

Support for Multi-valued Attributes. If a subject has more than one objects value for a particular property, then each distinct value is stored as a column name in the table for the row of that subject.

For now, this model still has some disadvantages. For complex query, there exists many table joins, which will reduce the efficiency of query. In the next two sections, we'll describe how to solve this problem.

4 Path Index in HBase

This section starts with an example. There is a SPARQL query that attempts to get all the graduate students who are now studying at the university from which they obtained their bachelor's degrees:

```
PREFIX rdf: <http://www.w3.org/1999/02/22-rdf-syntax-ns#>
PREFIX ub:
<http://www.lehigh.edu/~zhp2/2004/0401/univbench.owl#>
SELECT ?X ?Y ?Z
WHERE{
        ?X rdf:type ub:GraduateStudent .
        ?Y rdf:type ub:University .
        ?Z rdf:type ub:Department .
        ?X ub:memberOf ?Z .
        ?Z ub:subOrganizationOf ?Y .
        ?X ub:undergraduateDegreeFrom ?Y
}
```

For this query, the tables corresponding to three predicates (memberOf, subOrganizationOf, undergraduateDegreeFrom) will be accessed to get the results. Notice that there is a triangular relationship among the three variables X, Y and Z, as shown in Fig. 2 and thus will involve multi-table join among these three tables, which will be time consuming.

To reduce the cost of multi-table join when the query is complex, we propose *path index* based on our model. The core idea of path index is to construct some virtual predicates from the real predicates. Assuming there are two RDF triples graphically shown in Fig. 3, involving two predicates: *mem* and *sub*. These two predicates form a path of length two, from which a virtual predicate *mem_sub* is constructed. "Lecture1" is the subject of this new predicate and "University1" the object. However, we don't want to lose "Department1", which is the shared element among the initial two triples. We call this shared element *"join-ject"*, and store it in HBase too.

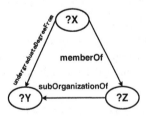
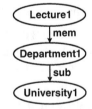

Fig. 2. Triangle query graph.   **Fig. 3.** RDF graph of two triples.

Virtual predicates is treated just the same as real predicates. Two tables (Pso, Pos) are created for each virtual predicates, too. In the Pso table for a virtual predicate, the subject is stored as row key and the concatenation of "join-ject" and object is stored as a column, which is different from table of real predicates. Similarly, in table Pos, a column is formed by the concatenation of "join-ject" and subject. The two tables of this example is shown in Table 2.

Table 2. Path index in HBase.

SO	
Row Key	**Columnfamily: cf**
Lecturer1	cf: (Department1, University1)

OS	
Row Key	**Columnfamily: cf**
University1	cf: (Department1, Lecturer1)

Path index can effectively reduce the number of joins by half in a complex query, thus enhancing efficiency. Both the data of real predicate and virtual predicate are stored twice based on vertical partitioning. Path index does not change the structure of our model, making the tables easy to manage. Path index is constructed using MapReduce on HBase tables. To construct a new table of a virtual predicate, we need two tables of real predicates, one as the input of *map*, the other as a look-up table in *reduce* phase.

5 Query Strategy

In this section we will discuss how to obtain efficient query based on our model.

A commonly used subset of SPARQL is the Basic Graph Pattern (BGP) queries of SPARQL, which consists of a set of triple patterns. For a triple pattern, if the predicate is a variable, it is necessary to query on all the tables in HBase. If the predicate is known, we only need to query on one particular table. There are total up to eight kinds of triple patterns and the table accessing strategy for each of these patterns is shown in Table 3.

Table 3. Table chosen for different triple pattern.

Triple Pattern	Strategy
S, P, O	Pso or Pos
?S, P, O	Pos
S, P, ?O	Pso
?S, P, ?O	Pso or Pos
S, ?P, O	Pso or Pos
?S, ?P, O	Pos
S, ?P, ?O	Pso
?S, ?P, ?O	Pso or Pos

For simple queries which consist of only a few triple patterns, the results can be obtained efficiently based on strategies in Table 3 using HBase API because there are few join operations in these queries. This is demonstrated in Sect. 6.

For complex queries which contain a few more triple patterns, path index is used to reduce the number of joins. Take the query represented by Fig. 2 for an example. There are three tables: mem (short for memberOf), sub (short for subOrganizationOf) and und (short for undergraduateDegreeFrom) that are to be joined. If path index is used, we can reduce that to two tables: mem_sub and und, in which mem_sub is the virtual predicate formed by mem and sub. Theoretically, assuming n is the number of triple patterns in a query, the number can be reduced to n/2 at best using path index, which will greatly improve the efficiency.

However, path index can only reduce the number of joins. It cannot eliminate joins. With the increase of data volume, the time consumed will increase linearly. MapReduce framework is adopted to deal with this problem, thus computing the results of joins in parallel. The query will be accomplished using n jobs and the output of job i is taken as the input of job $i + 1$. Each of the jobs accomplishes one or more joins in map phase. Our experiments show that the efficiency does not drop too fast when the data volume increases rapidly.

Rows are sorted alphabetically by the row key as they are stored in HBase tables, which allows our model to support range queries. HBase also supports filters such as regular expression filter applied on the server side instead of client side, which minimize unnecessary data transfers. For example, let us assume that one asks for all lecturers with telephone starting with "130" and the email address ending with "gmail.com". While retrieving the triples in the range [(telephone, 130), (telephone, 131)] in the Pos table, the server checks the email address of the corresponding lecturers and returns only those lecturers with Gmail address.

6 Experiments

For experiments, we used a cluster consisting of 1 Hadoop NameNode, 4 Hadoop DataNodes, 2 HBase Masters and 4 HBase RegionServers, with 1.81T configured capacity. Each Dell T410 node has 8-core Intel Xeon 2.40 GHz processor and 64 G RAM. We utilized the Lehigh University Benchmark (LUBM) [16] as a dataset of the experiment. As a benchmark for RDF data storage and query, LUBM describes the heterogeneous network between teachers, students and courses, etc.

Five dataset are tested on with the number of universities ranging from 1 to 600. As show in Table 4, the largest dataset D5 contains more than 82 million RDF triples. LUBM queries from 1 to 10 are used. Query 11, 12 and 13 are intended to verify the presence of certain OWL reasoning, which are not supported by our model. Query 14 is the simplest query which is similar to Query 6, so we just test on the first 10 queries.

Table 4. LUBM dataset.

	Number of Universities	RDF triple
D1	1	102707
D2	20	2873643
D3	100	14047872
D4	300	42104323
D5	600	82618021

6.1   Data Ingest

There are three methods to import data to HBase tables: HBase API, MapReduce that ingests data in reduce phase and MapReduce that ingests data in map phase, called map-side MapReduce. For the second method, we take predicate as the output key of map phase, thus the data for that predicate will be ingested to HBase by the corresponding reduce task.

Results are shown in Fig. 4, which shows that whatever methods is chosen, the time consumption increases linearly with the data volume increasing. Digesting in parallel is more efficient than in serial using HBase API. The second method consumes more time than the last method of map-side MapReduce. The reason is that for the second method, the data for one predicate are handled by a particular reduce task, which may lead to unbalanced load. In fact, there always exists one or more predicates of which the data are much larger than the data of most other predicates (In our experiments, about 50 times larger).

We also compare the space consumption for our model with Rya. HBase is used as the backend of Rya. The result (Fig. 5) shows that space consumed by Rya is nearly twice as much as our model.

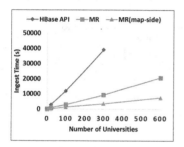
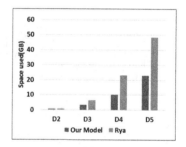

Fig. 4. Time consumption of data ingest.   **Fig. 5.** Space occupied by Rya and our model.

6.2   Query

10 queries (Q1 to Q10) are tested using the query strategy described in Sect. 5. We will discuss the efficiency of these queries according to the selectivity and complexity of the ten queries, which is shown in Table 5.

Table 5. Selectivity and complexity.

Query	Selectivity	Complexity
Q1, Q3, Q4, Q5, Q7, Q10	high	low
Q2, Q9	high	high
Q6	low	low
Q8	low	middle

For Q1, Q3, Q4, Q5, Q7 and Q10, which are simple and highly selective, the result is shown in Fig. 6. HBase demonstrates a gradual query time increase for these six queries when data become larger. The query time does not change much even when the data are hundred times larger. We also compare our model with Jena2 on the first three queries Q1, Q3 and Q5 of these six. The result (Fig. 7) shows the efficiency drops rapidly for Jena2 when data become larger. In comparison, these queries are efficient using our model.

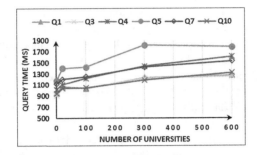

Fig. 6. Query time of Q1, Q3, Q4, Q5, Q7, and Q10.

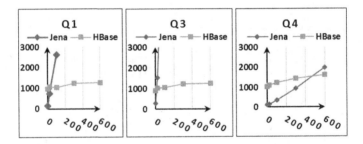

Fig. 7. Query time (ms) compared to Jena2.

For Q2, Q6, Q8 and Q9, the results (Fig. 8) are not as good as other queries. For Q2, Q6 and Q9, the query time grows linearly with the data volume increasing. There is a triangular pattern of relationships between the objects involved in both Q2 and Q9. Q2 asks for all graduate students who are members of a department that is a sub organization of the university they obtained their undergraduate degree from. Q9 asks for all the students who take the courses of their advisors, which is similar to Q2. Although path index can reduce the number of joins, when the RDF data reaches up to more than a billion triples, the efficiency will be very bad. Q6 asks for all the students, which is a very simple query but it returns a significantly large result set. The query time of query 6 grows rapidly because the return set grows rapidly when RDF data become larger. So the time consumption is a measure more of the network performance than that of the SPARQL query performance. Q8 is similar to Q6 in that it returns a large result set. But we can see the query time of Q8 doesn't grow that rapidly like Q6, which is because the result set does not change when RDF data become larger. To alleviate this, we try just returning the first 100 results for Q6 and Q8, and find that the efficiency becomes very good just like simple and highly selective query such as Q1.

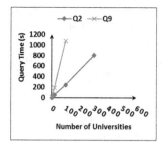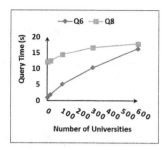

Fig. 8. Query time of Q2, Q6, Q8 and Q9.

To improve the efficiency of Q2 and Q9 which require multi-table joins, this paper propose to use cascading MapReduce that is described in Sect. 5. We run Q2 in parallel using this method and get the query time before and after optimization. As is shown in Fig. 9, query time for Q2 grows slowly after optimization. The time consumption on 80 million triples is only 15 % more than 40 million triples. But not all queris are efficient using MapReduce. Q1 is tested using MapReduce and the result shows that the efficiency becomes poorer. (Fig. 10).

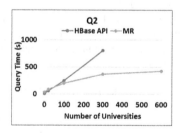

Fig. 9. Query time of Q2.   **Fig. 10.** Query time of Q1.

In this section, experiments are done on the performance of our model. The conclusion is that our model consumes less space in HBase compared to other model in the cloud and obtains good efficiency in data ingesting. Most queries can be efficiently accomplished using HBase API through strategies in Table 3. For other complex queries, cascading MapReduce jobs are needed to accomplish the joins.

7 Conclusion

In this paper, we presented a new RDF storage model using HBase. Based on HBase, we designed to store RDF triples into two types of tables. We proposed path index based on HBase to improve query performance and we described how to choose query strategies for different queries. Our model supports billions of triples and efficient queries.

Applications based on heterogeneous information network such as knowledge graph are drawing much attention of reseachers in related field. For future work, we plan on providing basic inference support for our model. We will investigate improvements of the RDF storage schema for HBase and incorporate Hive and Pig into our system to prefect our model. And we will research to support automatic choosing of optimal query strategy.

Acknowledgments. This work is supported in part by the National Key Basic Research and Department (973) Program of China (No. 2013CB329606), and the Co-construction Project of Beijing Municipal Commission of Education.

References

1. Yuanzhuo, W., Yantao, J., Dawei, L., Xiaolong, J., Xueqi, C.: Open web knowledge aided information search and data mining. J. Comput. Res. Dev. **52**(2), 456–474 (2015)
2. Du, F., Chen, Y.G., Du, X.Y.: Survey of RDF query processing techniques. Ruan Jian Xue Bao/J. Softw. **24**(6), 1222–1242 (2013)
3. Franke, C., Morin, S., Chebotko, A., Abraham, J., Brazier, P.: Distributed semantic web data management in HBase and MySQL cluster. In: IEEE International Conference on Cloud Computing (CLOUD), 2011, pp. 105–112. IEEE, July 2011
4. Abadi, D.J., Marcus, A., Madden, S.R., Hollenbach, K.: Scalable semantic web data management using vertical partitioning. In: Proceedings of the 33rd International Conference on Very Large Data Bases, pp. 411–422. VLDB Endowment, September 2007
5. Melnik, S.: Storing RDF in a relational database (2001)
6. Wilkinson, K., Wilkinson, K.: Jena property table implementation (2006)
7. Wilkinson, K., Sayers, C., Kuno, H.A., Reynolds, D.: Efficient RDF storage and retrieval in Jena2. In: SWDB, vol. 3, pp. 131–150, September 2003
8. Abadi, D.J., Marcus, A., Madden, S.R., Hollenbach, K.: SW-Store: a vertically partitioned DBMS for Semantic Web data management. VLDB J.—Int. J. Very Large Data Bases **18**(2), 385–406 (2009)
9. Kaoudi, Z., Manolescu, I.: RDF in the clouds: a survey. VLDB J. **24**(1), 1–25 (2014)
10. Husain, M.F., Doshi, P., Khan, L., Thuraisingham, B.: Storage and retrieval of large RDF graph using Hadoop and MapReduce. In: Jaatun, M.G., Zhao, G., Rong, C. (eds.) Cloud Computing. LNCS, vol. 5931, pp. 680–686. Springer, Heidelberg (2009)
11. Dittrich, J., Quiané-Ruiz, J.A., Jindal, A., Kargin, Y., Setty, V., Schad, J.: Hadoop ++: making a yellow elephant run like a cheetah (without it even noticing). Proc. VLDB Endow. **3**(1–2), 515–529 (2010)
12. Dittrich, J., Quiané-Ruiz, J.A., Richter, S., Schuh, S., Jindal, A., Schad, J.: Only aggressive elephants are fast elephants. Proc. VLDB Endow. **5**(11), 1591–1602 (2012)
13. Choi, H., Son, J., Cho, Y., Sung, M.K., Chung, Y.D.: SPIDER: a system for scalable, parallel/distributed evaluation of large-scale RDF data. In: Proceedings of the 18th ACM Conference on Information and Knowledge Management, pp. 2087–2088. ACM, November 2009
14. Sun, J., Jin, Q.: Scalable rdf store based on hbase and mapreduce. In: 2010 3rd International Conference on Advanced Computer Theory and Engineering (ICACTE), vol. 1, p. V1–633. IEEE, August 2010

15. Abraham, J., Brazier, P., Chebotko, A., Navarro, J., Piazza, A.: Distributed storage and querying techniques for a semantic web of scientific workflow provenance. In: IEEE International Conference on Services Computing (SCC), 2010, pp. 178–185. IEEE, July 2010

16. Guo, Y., Pan, Z., Heflin, J.: LUBM: a benchmark for OWL knowledge base systems. Web Semant. Sci. Serv. Agents World Wide Web **3**(2), 158–182 (2005)

17. Punnoose, R., Crainiceanu, A., Rapp, D.: SPARQL in the cloud using Rya. Inf. Syst. **48**, 181–195 (2015)

18. Broekstra, J., Kampman, A., van Harmelen, F.: Sesame: a generic architecture for storing and querying RDF and RDF schema. In: Horrocks, I., Hendler, J. (eds.) ISWC 2002. LNCS, vol. 2342, pp. 54–68. Springer, Heidelberg (2002)

19. Chong, E.I., Das, S., Eadon, G., Srinivasan, J.: An efficient SQL-based RDF querying scheme. In: VLDB, pp. 1216–1227, August 2005

20. Bornea, M.A., Dolby, J., Kementsietsidis, A., Srinivas, K., Dantressangle, P., Udrea, O., Bhattacharjee, B.: Building an efficient RDF store over a relational database. In: Proceedings of the 2013 ACM SIGMOD International Conference on Management of Data, pp. 121–132. ACM, 2013 June

21. Weiss, C., Karras, P., Bernstein, A.: Hexastore: sextuple indexing for semantic web data management. Proc. VLDB Endow. **1**(1), 1008–1019 (2008)

A New Link Prediction Algorithm
Based on Local Links

Juan Yang, Lixin Yang[(⊠)], and Pengye Zhang

Key Lab of Intelligent Telecommunication Software and Multimedia,
Beijing University of Posts and Telecommunications,
100876 Beijing, China
yangjuan@bupt.edu.cn, ylxsyf@163.com

Abstract. Link prediction refers to estimating the possibility of the existence of non-existent links between the nodes. The link prediction algorithms based on local information merely consider nodes' attributes or a small amount of topology information about common neighbors. In this paper, we proposed a new measure motivated by the cohesion between common neighbors and the predicted nodes——LNL (Local Neighbors Link). Experiments show that, compared with four classical algorithms on seven real networks, LNL has the higher accuracy and robustness. Furthermore, we apply the link prediction algorithms into large-scale networks. We implement the LNL method in both MapReduce and Spark, the experiments show that the implementation by Spark has higher efficiency than using MapReduce.

Keywords: Link prediction · Complex network · Adjacent nodes · Parallel algorithm · Spark

1 Introduction

Link Prediction is a key direction in complex network research, refers to estimating the possibility of the existence of non-existent links between node pairs according to the known network structure information [1]. It has been applied to the prediction of unknown information on protein network [2], relationship recommendation of microblogging users [3], evaluation of network evolving mechanisms [4], recommend collaborations [5], classification in partially labelled networks [6] and other fields.

The majority similarity-based link prediction algorithms are classified into several aspects: based on local, global and quasi-local information. Methods based on local information have lower time complexity, yet lower prediction accuracy, and may perform poorly on networks with different clustering coefficients. Global information considers longer paths of network instead of only nearest neighbors for sufficient information. Random walk link prediction algorithms calculate the probabilities of the

---

This work is supported in part by the National Key Basic Research and Department (973) Program of China (No. 2013CB329606), and the National Natural Science Foundation of China (No. 71231002, 61375058).

X. Xiao and Z. Zhang (Eds.): WAIM 2015, LNCS 9391, pp. 16–28, 2015.
DOI: 10.1007/978-3-319-23531-8_2

source node to the target node as the similarity between this node pair. The supervised learning methods transfer the link prediction problem into a classification problem. Both random walk and supervised learning methods are difficult to be parallelized.

The above works can handle specific networks; the approaches based on local information have the least time complexity. Considering the rapid growth of network, we focus on local information which is easy to be implemented and has low time cost. Meanwhile, link prediction has a broad applicability, the local index is simple but can be used in many ways, that is to say, it is worthy of improving its performance. Furthermore, we apply the link prediction algorithms based on common neighbors with adjacency information on large-scale networks. Thus, our researches focus on following problem:

1. Present a new approach LNL based on local links with better performances in accuracy and robustness.
2. Design the parallel LNL link prediction method, implement the parallel algorithm in both MapReduce and Spark, and compare their efficiency.

2 Related Work

Previous researches have investigated some classical algorithms: LP algorithm was introduced by Lü L et al. [7] with time complexity $O(Nk^3)$ (where N is the number of vertexes, k is time complexity to traverse the neighborhood of a node), this method based on CN method yet considering more path information within length 3. Katz [8] considered all the paths information which the shorter path has a higher weight. The usage of path information can make a good prediction for sparse networks of both Katz and LP methods, yet the computational complexity is high. Prediction with random walk has several indices including LWR [9], SWR [9] et al., and the integral accuracy is high. Mohammad A H et al. [10] transformed link prediction problem into classification problem, the method extracted a set of features of network as input for supervised learning for link prediction. Fire M et al. [11] took topological features for supervised learning, and ranked the importance of each feature.

Comparing with the above methods, the approaches based on local information have the least time complexity and broad applicability. This paper focuses on the algorithms based on local information including: Common Neighbors (CN), Jaccard [12], Adamic-Adar (AA) [13], PA [14], RA [15]. CN takes the number of common neighbors as the existing possibility of nodes. On the basis of CN, AA and RA improve the accuracy by assigning the less connected neighbors more weight. The similarity index AA is defined as: $S_{xy} = \sum_{z \in \Gamma(x) \cap \Gamma(y)} 1/logk(z)$, $k(z)$ represents the degree of node z, $\Gamma(x)$ is the neighbor of node x. AA refines the nodes with lower degree have more weight. RA has a similar form with AA while it decays faster, RA is motivated by the resource allocation process taking place on networks with definition: $S_{xy} = \sum_{z \in \Gamma(x) \cap \Gamma(y)} 1/k(z)$. Compared with AA, RA performs better [4] in most cases. Connecting possibility of x and y is proportional to their degree in PA, namely $S_{xy} = k(x) \cdot k(y)$. Noted that PA requires less information which has the least computational complexity, yet the performance is very poor in the highly clustered network.

Recent research found that clustering coefficient of networks has a large impact on link prediction algorithms' applicability [4], some algorithms focus on topological characteristic have been developed. In 2011, Dong Y. X et al. [16] designed a new algorithm IA exploiting the interactions between common neighbors defined as:$S_{xy} = \sum_{z \in \Gamma(x) \cap \Gamma(y)} e_z / k(z)$, where e_z refers to the links between z and other common neighbors of x and y. It proved well performance while maintain low time complexity. Another method LCP accounts for the singular topology was proposed [17], the connecting possibility of node pairs is strictly limited, it has a great accuracy in precision, but not satisfactory in overall accuracy evaluation.

Classified similarity indexes cannot distinguish the importance of common neighbors when the node pair shares no more than two common neighbors while it is common in many networks. This paper puts forward a new index based on local neighbors' link degree——LNL (Local Neighbors Link) index, considering both attribute and topological features between the target points' adjacent nodes and their common neighbors. Extensive experiments on disparate real world networks demonstrate that LNL outperformed existing algorithms. In the next section, we will present the LNL index in detail. In Sect. 4, the parallel implementation is designed for link prediction algorithms. In Sect. 5, the experimental result of LNL will be compared with previous methods; compare the parallel performance between MapReduce and Spark.

3   Local Neighbors Link Method

Given an undirected network G (V, E), where V presents the set of nodes, E is the set of edges, e_{wv} refers to the link between w and v. There is no loopback in the network. Link Prediction refers to calculate the possibility of the existence of non-existent links between node pairs.

In Fig. 1, for the classical algorithms CN, AA and RA, c1 and c2 are treated respectively the same weight in Fig. 1 (a) and (b), therefore S_{xy} is same in Fig. 1 (a) and (b). However, we can observe from Fig. 1 that (take c1 as examples):

(1) In Fig. 1 (a), c1 has total four links with neighbors of x and y (include x and y), yet in Fig. 1 (b) c1's friends are all neighbors of x and y (include x and y). That is to say, c1 in Fig. 1 (b) may have more contact with x and y than in Fig. 1 (a).
(2) Walk from x to y, there exist three paths passed c1 that length less than three in Fig. 1 (a), in contrast, there exist five paths passed c1 in Fig. 1 (b), namely, x and y have more possibilities to connect each other by passing c1 in Fig. 1 (b).

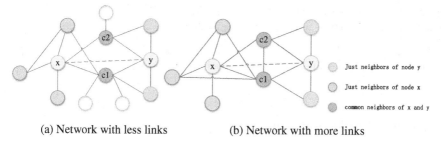

(a) Network with less links   (b) Network with more links

Fig. 1. Example network: x and y are the predicted nodes, c1 and c2 are the common neighbors of x and y, S_{xy} is the link probability of x and y.

LNL is motivated by the cohesion between common neighbors and the predicted nodes. The predicted node pair is x and y, c is one of their common neighbors; $k(c)$ is the degree of c. The basic idea is that if c has more links with the predicted nodes occupied $k(c)$, more weight will be assigned to c.

It should cover the above observation: (1) if c has more common friends with the predicted nodes occupied its total friends, meaning that it may have more contact with the predicted node pairs. (2) If c has more common friends, refers to c will generate more possibilities for the connections between x and y, for it provides more paths within 3 steps. Thus the weight of c is defined as:

$$w(c) = \frac{\sum_{v \in \Gamma(x) \cup x} \delta(c, v) + \sum_{w \in \Gamma(y) \cup y} \delta(c, w)}{k(c)} \qquad (1)$$

Where $\Gamma(x)$ is the set of neighbor of node x, $\Gamma(y)$ is the set of neighbors of node y, the $\delta(w, v)$ represents whether there exist a link between w and v which is defined as:

$$\delta(w, v) = \begin{cases} 0 & e_{wv} \notin E \\ 1 & e_{wv} \in E \end{cases} \qquad (2)$$

If there is no link between w and v, $\delta(w, v) = 0$, conversely $\delta(w, v) = 1$. Compared Eq. 1 with existing CN, AA and RA, a main difference in assigning weight for c is that Eq. 1 considering second-order neighbors information instead of merely nearest common neighbors.

S_{xy} is the accumulation of each common neighbor c, the definition of LNL index as:

$$S_{xy} = \sum_{c \in \Gamma(x) \cap \Gamma(y)} w(c) \qquad (3)$$

In Eq. 3 suggests that x and y have more common friends, S_{xy} will get higher scores by accumulating each weight of common neighbors. Take Fig. 1 as an example, S_{xy} is calculated by LNL index as:

Figure 1 (a): $S_{xy} = w(c1) + w(c2) = (2+2)/6 + (1+2)/4 = 17/12$;
Figure 1 (b): $S_{xy} = w(c1) + w(c2) = (4+3)/6 + (2+3)/4 = 29/12$;

The result from (b) is greater than (a), the LNL is proved to distinguish the possibility of (a) and (b), while other indices such as CN, AA and RA are generally not available in this situation.

4 Parallel Implementation

To apply link prediction into large complex network, this paper design and implements a parallel method based on existing parallel method [19]. Existing parallel link prediction algorithm based on local information using MapReduce [18, 19] is proposed in 2012, this method can process large scale network of millions nodes, it proved to be $O(N/U)$ time complexity, where N is the number of nodes, U is the number of processing units. However, it doesn't give clear solutions to dealing the link prediction with additional common neighbors' information, thus we design a pre-process of carrying additional attributes for common neighbors. Besides, MapReduce is not good at multiple job execution for it will cost more starting time. A parallel programming model named Spark [20] will be used to implement the parallel link prediction and compared its efficiency with the implementation by MapReduce.

4.1 Spark

In MapReduce, each job need to reload the data from the disk which produced by Map task, it is time-consuming. While Spark outperforms MapReduce in iterative jobs for its memory computing which can save read/write time and starting time.

Furthermore, the parallelization is transparent to the developers and easy to implement. Spark provides two abstractions for the programming, RDD and parallel operations on datasets. The developer only needs to implement the high-level control flow of the application and launches various operations in parallel.

4.2 Link Prediction Parallelization

We design the implementation of parallel link perdition that enhance the applicability, apart from the classical link prediction such as CN,AA, RA et al. (except PA), it can handle the many similarity-based algorithms such as IA, LNL et al. which require common neighbors' additional attributes like neighbors or degree information.

The adjacency information can be saved in a file, and be read into the relevant Map task, however, some large-scale networks are too large to be read into memory. For link prediction algorithm in this paper which frequently query the attributes about common neighbors which needs O (1) query time complexity. We design a parallel pre-process to keep them in memory. The whole pseudo code of link prediction is divided into three parts as follows:

(1) Pre-process Parallelization

```
Input: <X, Y> :<X, Y>   E from G (V, E)
Output: <X, Q(info)[1~n]> : Q(info)[1~n] is the
neighbors of node X with additional information
(Output)
Calculate the adjacent nodes Q[1~n] for each node X
begin
   var i := 0;
   repeat
      EMIT(Q[i], X(Q[1~n]))
      i:= i + 1
   until i:= n
end.
Calculate the adjacent neighbors carrying additional
information Q(info)[1~n] for each node X
```

(2) Parallel the predicted node pairs using literature [19], the main pseudo code as follows

```
Input: <X,Q(info)[1~n]> : defined as above mentioned
Output: <(X,Z),S_ (X, Z)> : (x, Z) is one node pair,
S_(X, Z) is weight of one common neighbors
begin
   var i := 0; j:=0; score=0;
   newpair: String Input
   repeat
      repeat
         j:=i+1
         newpair:= sorted Order(Q[i],Q[j])
         score : =Similarity(X,Q(info)[i],Q(info)[j])
         EMIT(newpair, score)
         j:= j+1
      until j:= n
   until i:= n-1
end.
```

(3) **Parallel the accumulation of score fragments**

```
Input: <(X,Z),S[1~k]> : (x, Z) is one node pair, S[i]
is the weight of i-th common neighbors, total k common
neighbors
Output: <(X, Z), S(X, Z)> : S(X, Z) prediction score
of (X, Z)
begin
    var i := 0; sum :=0;
    repeat
        sum := sum + S[i]
        i:= i + 1
    until i:= k
    EMIT((X, Z), sum)
end.
```

Time Complexity: The first part is to compute the adjacent neighbors of nodes, the time complexity is $O(Nk)$, where N is the number of nodes and k is the average degree of nodes. According to literature [19], there are $k(k-1)/2$ node pairs for every common neighbor. Algorithms for LNL, it needs to compute the link between common neighbors and the predicted node pairs, suppose common neighbors respectively have average m and n links, the computational complexity is $O((l^2 + m^2)k^2)$ for one

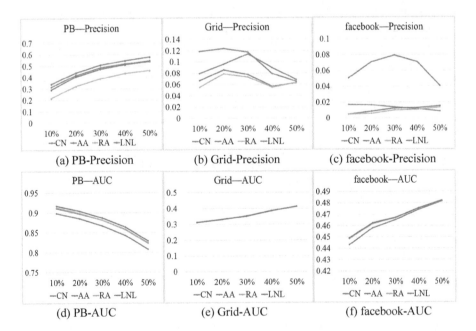

Fig. 2. Comparison about robustness of three real network with different ratio of E_t and E_p.

common neighbors, furthermore, $O(N(l^2 + m^2)k^2)$ for all the nodes. Last step is to accumulate the score of each node pair, supposed d is average number of common neighbors, the accumulated time is $O(Nd)$, the total time complexity is $O(N((l^2 + m^2)k^2 + d + k))$. Suppose the splits parameter of the data is K, then the time complexity is $O(N((l^2 + m^2)k^2 + d + k)/K)$, the higher of K, the shorter running time.

5 Experiments

5.1 Data

In this paper, we compare LNL with CN, AA, RA, and IA four classical algorithms, take standard evaluation method Precision and AUC. Also consider seven representative networks including: C.elegans [21], USAir [22], Grid [21], PB [23], Yeast [24], ego-facebook [25] and H.friendships [26]. Table 1 summarizes the basic topological features of these networks. N and M are the total numbers of nodes and links, respectively. C is the clustering coefficient, <d> is the average path length, <k> refer to the average degree of the network. Literature [4] concludes that clustering coefficient has high representative of link prediction algorithms. Consequently, we choose seven networks with comprehensive coverage of different types and clustering coefficient.

In order to test the algorithms' accuracy, the exist links E is divided into two parts: the training set E_t and the probe set E_p, where $E = E_t + E_p$. In the experiments, we use the classical evaluation methods Precision [27] and AUC [28].

To test the performance of parallel link prediction, we choose four large scale datasets from different type of network provide by Stanford Large Network Dataset Collection [29]. The detailed information about the datasets are described in Table 2.

Table 1. Topological features of representative networks.

Network	N	M	C	<d>	<k>
C.elegans	297	2,359	0.308	2.455	14.465
USAir	332	2,126	0.749	2.738	12.807
Grid	4,941	6,595	0.107	18.756	2.67
PB	1,490	19,090	0.36	2.738	27.312
Yeast	2,361	7,182	0.2	4.376	5.63
ego-facebook	2,888	2,981	0.803	3.867	2.064
H.friendships	1,858	12,534	0.167	3.453	13.491

Table 2. Topological features of large-scale networks

ID	Network	N	M	C	Type
D1	ca-HepTh	9877	25998	0.4714	Collaboration networks
D2	email-Enron	36692	183831	0.497	Communication networks
D3	DBLP	317080	1049866	0.6324	Networks with ground-truth communities
D4	roadNet-PA	1088092	1541898	0.0465	Road networks

5.2　Accuracy

In the experiments, we randomly select the training set E_t (contains 90 % links) and the probe set E_p (contains 10 % links), repeated ten times the experiment to calculate the average accuracy, averages is taken to four decimal places. In Precision evaluation method, L takes 100. In AUC method, we randomly select the compare pairs N = 20,000,000 times.

As evidenced in Table 3, apart from USAir, LNL achieves more accurate predictions than other existing algorithms, especially significant improvement for ego-facebook and H.friends. From the experimental results in Table 3, LNL has a better performance in sparse network, since LNL consider a wider range of connections between nodes instead of just common neighbors, it differs the contribution of each common neighbor. Table 4 shows the result evaluated by AUC, LNL maintain the optimum of accuracy except USAir. The accuracy of USAir is not the optimal but the difference in an acceptable range, that is to say, LNL proved to be the better methods and perform better.

Table 3. Accuracies of five similarity indices, measured by Precision method

Precision	C.elegans	USAir	Grid	PB	Yeast	ego-facebook	H.friends
CN	0.123	0.607	0.0890	0.4090	0.2020	0.017	0.0230
AA	0.132	0.623	0.0630	0.3610	0.1880	0.008	0.0170
RA	0.126	**0.636**	0.0530	0.2230	0.1530	0.007	0.0110
IA	0.138	0.624	0.1070	0.4510	0.2740	0.007	0.0240
LNL	**0.149**	0.63	**0.1200**	**0.4540**	**0.2920**	**0.067**	**0.1090**

Table 4. Accuracies of five similarity indices, measured by AUC method

AUC	C.elegans	USAir	Grid	PB	Yeast	ego-facebook	H.friends
CN	0.7877	0.9204	0.3144	0.9003	0.5146	0.4427	0.6732
AA	0.8345	0.9412	0.3145	0.9124	0.5168	0.4487	0.6831
RA	0.8380	**0.9473**	0.3145	0.9134	0.5167	0.4488	0.6837
IA	0.8392	0.9444	0.3145	0.9139	0.5168	0.4487	0.6842
LNL	**0.8457**	0.9405	**0.3145**	**0.9186**	**0.5174**	**0.4493**	**0.6888**

5.3　Robustness

To test the robustness of LNL, we choose three real networks: PB, Grid, ego-facebook and compared with CN, AA, RA indices. We randomly select the training set E_t and the probe set E_p, E_t from 90 % to 50 % decrease by 10 %, accordingly, E_p from 10 % ~ 50 % increase in 10 %, repeated ten times the experiment to calculate the average accuracy. The parameter N is set as the previous section described. L takes 20 % probes set links (If L is lower than 100, then L takes 100) for considering widely for the larger test set.

Figure 2 (a) demonstrates that the prediction accuracy increased with the proportional change of E_t and E_p, and LNL perform best overall. In Fig. 2 (b), besides CN, other algorithms achieve the peak in 20 % ratio for Grid, through 10 %–50 %, LNL get the highest precision. For ego-facebook network, LNL reach the peak at 30 %, and the accuracy is significantly higher than other methods. In terms of AUC, except PB decrease along with the increase of E_p, the others increase oppositely, LNL maintain the optimum of accuracy. Therefore, with different proportion of E_t and E_p, LNL performs best comparing with the others, thus it is quite robustness.

Time Complexity: The computational complexity of CN is $O(Nk^2)$ (where N is the total number of nodes, k is the average number of neighbors), AA and RA is consistent with CN in complexity. IA has a time complexity of $O(Nk^2 + Nkn^2)$ (n is the number of links between one common neighbors and other common neighbors). LNL respectively computes the number of links between common neighbor c and predicted x and y, it cost $O(Nkl^2 + Nkm^2)$ (where l is the total links of c and x, m is the total links of c and y), thus the computational complexity is $O(Nk^2 + Nkl^2 + Nkm^2)$.

5.4   Efficiency of Parallelization

Cluster Setup: We ran the large scale experiments on 5-node Hadoop cluster. Hadoop version is 2.20. Every node has the same hardware configuration: Dual CPU, 24-core, 64G of memory, configuration about each core: Intel(R) Xeon(R) CPU E5-2620 v2 @ 2.10 GHz. In the experiments: K refers to the data split number, for Spark, K is the parallels parameter; for MapReduce, K is the Reduce number.

Performance: We first implement the parallel link prediction by Map Reduce, and analyze its performance. In map Reduce, we totally generate three Jobs of this algorithm. The first Job is to generate the adjacent information of each node; the second Job need to produce all node pairs and compute the score of each common neighbor. The last Job is to accumulate the final prediction score of each node pair.

As shown in Fig. 3 (a), the X-axis is the parallel parameter K, Y-axis is the running time (Minute). Running time decreases sharply with the increasing of K by 4 steps. We also record the inter-bytes (M) of the algorithms as Fig. 3 (b) shown. Compare Fig. 3 (a) with Fig. 3 (b), we can notice that the running time is proportional to the inter-bytes.

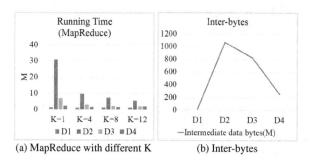

(a) MapReduce with different K   (b) Inter-bytes

Fig. 3. Running time of MapReduce with different K, K represents the number of data splits.

And the space complexity of LNL is $S(Nk^2)$, its inter-bytes are proportional to the N and k (where k is the average degree of the network).

MapReduce vs Spark: We implement the parallel link prediction in both MapReduce and Spark. As evidenced in Fig. 4, we observe that the running time of Spark is shorter than MapReduce, the running time is less than 50 % for most datasets with the same parameter K >=4. The reason for the difference can be explained as follows: (1) Spark is based on memory computation, while MapReduce need to write its inter-bytes into the local disk in Map task and reload in the Reduce task. It will cost I/O read/write time especially performs badly for large inter-bytes. (2) Spark only needs to start one time the Job of the link prediction algorithm, while the MapReduce needs to start three times. This case cannot represent the typical examples of iterative operation, but it still reduces the running time for using Spark.

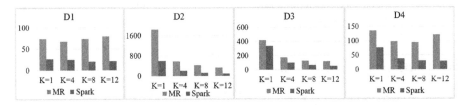

Fig. 4. MapReduce vs Spark on running time: the left Y-axis is the running time (seconds), and the X-axis is the parallel parameter K. D1, D2, D3, D4 are the four networks.

6   Conclusion and Future Work

This paper proposed a new index based on local neighbors links——LNL (Local Neighbors Link), in which attributes and topological connections between nodes are considered. We empirically compared some prediction algorithms. Numerical results of seven real networks shows that LNL outperformed in accuracy. Besides, we design the parallel pre-process of link prediction to enhance applicability of existing method [19]. We improve its efficiency by implementing LNL in a parallel programming model named Spark, and the experiments show that the performance is better by using Spark than MapReduce for large-scale networks.

The research about LNL may be used as topological features for supervised learning of better link prediction accuracy.

References

1. Getoor, L., Diehl, C.P.: Link mining: a survey. ACM SIGKDD Explor. Newslett. **7**(2), 3–12 (2005)
2. Li, J., Shang, X.Q., Guo, Y., Li, X.Y.: New approach of link prediction in PPI network. Appl. Res. Comput. **11**, 016 (2012)

3. Wu, M.: Research on Relationship recommender systems based on link prediction, Beijing University of Posts and Telecommunications (2012)
4. Lü, L., Zhou, T.: Link prediction in complex networks: a survey. Physica A **390**(6), 1150–1170 (2011)
5. Guns, R., Rousseau, R.: Recommending research collaborations using link prediction and random forest classifiers. Scientometrics **101**(2), 1461–1473 (2014)
6. Zhang, Q., Shang, M., Lü, L.: Similarity-based classification in partially labeled networks. Int. J. Mod. Phys. C **21**(06), 813–824 (2010)
7. Lü, L., Jin, C.H., Zhou, T.: Similarity index based on local paths for link prediction of complex networks. Phys. Rev. E **80**(4), 046122 (2009)
8. Katz, L.: A new status index derived from sociometric analysis. Psychometrika **18**(1), 39–43 (1953)
9. Liu, W., Lü, L.: Link prediction based on local random walk. EPL (Europhy. Lett.) **89**(5), 58007 (2010)
10. Al Hasan, M., Chaoji, V., Salem, S., Zaki, M.: Link prediction using supervised learning. In: SDM 2006: Workshop on Link Analysis, Counter-terrorism and Security (2006)
11. Fire, M., Tenenboim, L., Lesser, O., Puzis, R., Rokach, L., Elovici, Y.: Link prediction in social networks using computationally efficient topological features. In: 2011 IEEE Third International Conference on Privacy, Security, Risk and Trust (PASSAT) and 2011 IEEE Third Inernational Conference on Social Computing (SocialCom), pp. 73–80. IEEE (2011)
12. Jaccard, P.: Etude comparative de la distribution florale dans une portion des Alpes et du Jura. Impr. Corbaz. (1901)
13. Adamic, L.A., Adar, E.: Friends and neighbors on the Web. Soc. Netw. **25**(3), 211–230 (2003)
14. Barabási, A., Albert, R.: Emergence of scaling in random networks. Science **286**(5439), 509–512 (1999)
15. Zhou, T., Lü, L., Zhang, Y.C.: Predicting missing links via local information. Eur. Phy. J. B. **71**(4), 623–630 (2009)
16. Dong, Y.X., Ke, Q., Wu, B.: Link prediction based on node similarity. Comput. Sci. **38**(7), 162 (2011)
17. Cannistraci, C.V., Alanis-Lobato, G., Ravasi, T.: From link-prediction in brain connectomes and protein interactomes to the local-community-paradigm in complex networks. Scientific reports, 3 (2013)
18. Dean, J., Ghemawat, S.: MapReduce: simplified data processing on large clusters. Commun. ACM. **51**(1), 107–113 (2008)
19. Rao, J., Wu, B., Dong, Y.X.: Parallel link prediction in complex network using MapReduce. Ruanjian Xuebao/J. Softw. **23**(12), 3175–3186 (2012)
20. Zaharia, M., Chowdhury, M., Franklin, M.J., Shenker, S., Stoica, I.: Spark: cluster computing with working sets. In: Proceedings of the 2nd USENIX Conference on Hot Topics in Cloud Computing, pp. 10–10 (2010)
21. Watts, D.J., Strogatz, S.H.: Nature **393**, 440–442 (1998)
22. Batagelj, V., Mrvar, A.: Pajek datasets (2006). http://vlado.fmf.uni-lj.si/pub/networks/data/mix/USAir97.net
23. Adamic, L.A., Glance, N.: The political blogosphere and the 2004 US election: divided they blog. In: Proceedings of the 3rd International Workshop on Link Discovery, pp. 36–43. ACM (2005)
24. Vladimir Batagelj and Andrej Mrvar (2006): Pajek datasets. http://vlado.fmf.uni-lj.si/pub/networks/data/bio/Yeast/Yeast.htm
25. Facebook (NIPS) network dataset – {KONECT} (2015)
26. Hamsterster friendships network dataset – {KONECT} (2015)

27. Herlocker, J.L., Konstan, J.A., Terveen, L.G., Riedl, J.T.: Evaluating collaborative filtering recommender systems. ACM Trans. Inf. Syst. (TOIS) **22**(1), 5–53 (2004)
28. Hanley, J.A., McNeil, B.J.: The meaning and use of the area under a receiver operating characteristic (ROC) curve. Radiology **143**(1), 29–36 (1982)
29. Leskovec J. Stanford large network dataset collection. http://snap.stanford.edu/data/

Spammer Detection on Online Social Networks Based on Logistic Regression

Xiang Zhu[✉], Yuanping Nie, Songchang Jin, Aiping Li, and Yan Jia

College of Computer, National University of Defense Technology,
Changsha, China
zhuxiang@nudt.edu.cn, {yuanpingnie,apli1974}@gmail.com,
jsc04@126.com, jiayanjy@vip.sina.com

Abstract. Millions of users generate and propagate information in online social network. Search engines and data mining tools allow people to track hot topics and events online. However, the massive use of social media also makes it easier for malicious users, known as social spammers, to occupy social network with junk information. To solve this problem, a classifier is needed to detect social spammers. One effective way for spammer detection is based on contents and user information. Nevertheless, social spammers are tricky and able to fool the system with evolving their contents and information. Firstly, social spammers continually change their patterns to deceive detecting system. Secondly, spammers will try to gain influence and disguise themselves as far as possible. Due to the dynamic pattern of social spammers, it is difficult for existing methods to effectively and efficiently respond to social spammers. In this paper, we present a model based on logistic regression considering content attributes and behavior attributes of users in social network. Analyses of user attributes are made to differentiate spammers and non-spammers inherently. Experimental results on Twitter data show the effectiveness and efficiency of the proposed method.

Keywords: Social network · Social spammer · Classifier · Logistic regression

1 Introduction

Online social networks, like Facebook and Twitter, are increasingly used in many fields such as education, marketing and politics. While social network has become important platform for information diffusion and communication, it has also become disgraceful for social spammers who publish and propagate junk information. The flood of social spammers seriously influence the experience of normal accounts, detecting social spammers can make a great contribution to the development of online social network. It will promote the user experience and healthy use of the whole online social network.

X. Zhu—Sponsored by National Key fundamental Research and Development Program No. 2013CB329601.

© Springer International Publishing Switzerland 2015
X. Xiao and Z. Zhang (Eds.): WAIM 2015, LNCS 9391, pp. 29–40, 2015.
DOI: 10.1007/978-3-319-23531-8_3

Traditional spammer detecting methods become less effective due to the fast evaluation of social spammers. Social spammers try to disguise themselves as normal users by changing information and dynamic patterns to cheat the system. In order to detect social spammers effectively, it is necessary to build a new model to take new characters into account. There are differences between social spammers and normal users in attributes and behaviors. Normal users will be more active than social spammers, which is reflected in their content attributes and user information. Social spammers disguise themselves as normal users generally, but when they launch attacks, their behavior patterns will be abnormal. So it is possible to take advantage of those factors which differentiate social spammers from normal users to build a classifier for spammer detection.

The rest of the paper is organized as follows. The next Section introduce the background and related work of spammer detection in social network, several existing methods are presented. In Sect. 3, crawling strategy and labeled collection build method are depicted in detail. Then a classifier based on logistic regression model considering attributes and behaviors is introduced. Section 4 selects several evaluation metrics and makes comparison experiments using crawled data with existing methods, the ability to distinguish spammers and non-spammers is investigated. Section 5 makes conclusions and orientation of the future work.

2   Background and Related Work

Online social networks have become the preferred form of communication not only between friends and family, but also in business affairs. Friends and family members will share the life information and communicate with each other in online social networks. In order to increase exposure of a brand, a lots of traditional shops build their accounts online to introduce their products and hold business campaign. It will attract people to participate in the activity and discuss about it, all the behaviors will make contributions to information diffusion. Social networks are important platforms for information diffusion and communication. However, they have also become infamous for spammers who overwhelm normal users with junk information. These fake accounts, known as social spammers, are a special kind of users in social media. They cooperate among themselves as a union to launch various attacks such as advertisement dissemination to increase sales, propagating pornography, viruses and phishing and then secretly steal normal users' information. The problem of social spammer is a serious issue in many aspects. Detecting and combating social spammers can significantly improve user experience in a social network and promote the healthy and safety of the whole social media environment.

Spammer detection has been applied in various fields, including email system [4], information retrieval system [8], video websites [2] and online social networks [1]. Following the spammer detection technologies in email system, a lot of efforts are devoted to detecting spammers in various social network websites, including twitter, facebook, sina weibo, etc. A lot of detection and combating strategies are proposed to solve the problem [5,6,11,12]. Existing methods can be divided into two categories. The first kind of method is based on contents analysis. Content attributes and user behavior attributes [1] are used to tell spammers from normal users. Users' profile information and behavior patterns are extracted to build filter model. Another category is based on social structure. A hypothesis of those methods is that social spammers cannot establish social relationship with normal users widely. The users with relatively low social influence and social relationship will be classified into spammer category.

Traditional spammer detecting methods become less effective because of the fast evaluation of social spammers and large scale of information in online social network. Firstly, social spammers have dynamic behavior patterns. Spammers change posting strategies continuously to behave like a normal user. Spammers will copy normal user's tweets or repost their tweets to pretend normal users to deceive system. Secondly, spammers will try to gain social influence by following normal users deliberately. The users followed by spammers maybe follow spammers back and social spammers will unfollow users who does not follow themselves periodically to keep them looking like regular. Thus, due to the rapidly evolving characteristics, it is necessary to build a framework to reflect dynamic patterns of social spammers.

3   Spammer Detection Approach

In order to evaluate performance of our approach in spammer detection on online social networks, we need a labeled collection, in which users are pre-classified into spammers and non-spammers. To the best of our knowledge, no appropriate collection is publicly available, so we need to build one. In Sect. 3.1, we represent the method to build a labeled collection. Then we identify user's attributes and discuss the process to manually classify a set of spammers and non-spammers in Sect. 3.2. In Sect. 3.3, we propose a method Attribute and Behavior Logistic Regression (ABLR), based on Logistic Regression Model to detect spammers.

3.1   Dataset and Label Collection

Twitter is an online social networking service which enables users to send and read short text messages (i.e. tweets) that appear on their friends pages. Users in Twitter are identified only by a screen name which cannot be changed and, optionally, by a real name which can be changed. Users can submit a photo as their profile image, otherwise their profile image will be a default photo. To profile a user, it is possible to analyze the attributes, such as the tweets he sends, the users he follows and the followers of him etc.

Sina Weibo is a Chinese microblogging (weibo) website. Akin to a hybrid of Facebook and Twitter, it is one of the most popular sites in China. A great deal of active users update their messages, repost interesting messages and establish friendships in Sina Weibo. We can also analyze users in Sina Weibo, the attributes of the users in Sina Weibo are similar to the attributes in Twitter.

Fortunately, both Twitter and Sina Weibo provide API for developers to crawl users' information. We launch our crawler on those online social networks to collect users' information such as user's profile image, the number of messages updated, the time of the last message, the number of followers or friends and so on. Those attributes will make contributions to the spammer detection, we can tell spammers account from normal human beings account by taking advantages of the attributes.

Next, we describe the procedure to build our labeled collection. There are some properties that need to be taken into account to create a suitable collection for training. First of all, the collection needs to have a sufficient number of spammers and non-spammers. Secondly, the number of spammers and the number of non-spammers should be in the same magnitude. Thirdly, it is desirable that each group of users are chosen randomly from the social networks.

Table 1. Statistics of the Datasets

Attribute	Value
The number of spammers	35150
The number of human beings	16125
The number of tweets	1,452,437

In order to meet our desired properties, we take the following strategy to build labeled collection. First, we can get a list of celebrities' profile in which the user has more than 10,000 followers [13]. There are 6,499 celebrities in total and we can add them to non-spammers collection reasonably. Then, we set our crawler to those celebrities to get their followers randomly. Finally, we get a made-up data set including 51,275 users. The detailed information about the datasets is shown in Table 1.

3.2   Identifying User Attributes

Unlike normal users, spammers in online social networks aim at commercial intent (e.g. advertising) and engage in campaign online. Since spammers and non-spammers have different goals in online social network, we expect they have different behaviors to achieve their purposes. Intuitively, we suppose that non-spammers spend more time interacting with other users. for example, they post tweets without URL, reply other user's tweet, repost other user's tweet and so on. While spammers' performance is intermittent and inactive compared with non-spammers. In order to verify our hypothesis, we focus on characteristics of the users in data set. We analyze a large set of attributes reflecting users' behavior that distinguishing spammers from non-spammers.

In the interest of distinguishing spammers from non-spammers, we consider two kind of attributes, content attributes and behavior attributes [1]. Content attributes include properties of messages posted by users (e.g. tweet, reply and repost) and attributes of users (e.g. the number of friends, followers and tweets). Given the content attributes, we analyze content characteristics based on following metrics: total number of tweets, number of URLs of each tweet, number of friends of a user, number of followers of a user, follower friend ratio (FFR), type of a user. Next, we observe four characteristics of content attributes that can differ spammers from non-spammers: number of followers, number of friends, FFR, number of tweets.

Figure 1 shows cumulative distribution function (CDF) of content attributes. In Fig. 1(a), we can find that non-spammer users have more followers than spammer users. Intuitively non-spammer users have more social relationship in real world, so they will get followers easily. The number of followers of most spammer users are lower than 100, because the majority of spammers are inactive with other users in social network. In Fig. 1(b), the CDF curves show the difference in the number of friends between non-spammers and spammers. Obviously, non-spammers' friends are more than spammers' friends in the mass. Because non-spammers interact with others more frequently, they will follow others if they get interested in those users. The difference between Fig. 1(b) and (a) is that the nubmer of friends of most spammers are more than 100 for the reason following a user is one-way operation. Figure 1(c) displays FFR of spammers and non-spammers, we can observe that FFR of non-spammers is higher than FFR of spammers in general. The FFR of most spammers are lower than 1, which means the number of followers is less than the number of friends. We can notice in the non-spammers' curve, most non-spammers' FFR are close to 1 for the reason most acquaintance in real world will follow each other in social network and will not follow users they are not familiar with. Figure 1(d) demonstrates the CDF curves of total number of tweets. The situation is similar to Fig. 1(a), non-spammers are more active than spammers in the mass, non-spammers update tweets more frequently than spammers.

Behavior attributes consist of behavior model of users, posting frequence and social interactions. We consider following metrics as behavior attributes: days away from system, number of times the user was mentioned, number of times the user mention others, self-similarity of user's tweets [14,16], age of the user account. We pick two characteristics to analyze user's behavior attributes: days away from system, self-similarity of user's tweets.

Figure 2(a) shows CDF curves of user's days away from system. We calculate days according to the date of user's latest tweet and the date we check it. We can notice that more than 60 percent non-spammers are not away from system exceed 10 days, that means non-spammers will keep active persistently for a long time. While more than 30 percent spammers are away from system exceed about 250 days. Specially, the uprush in spammers' curve is due to the fact that about 40 percent spammers never post any tweets, so we set the days away from system to 365 artificially. Figure 2(b) demonstrates CDF curves of self-similarity of user's tweets. We sample 200 tweets from user's tweets and calculate self-similarity score [14], self-similarity score ranges from 0 to 1. Figure 2(b) shows 80 percent non-spammers have lower self-similarity score than 0.01, while more than 30 percent spammers get a higher self-similarity score than 0.2. That is

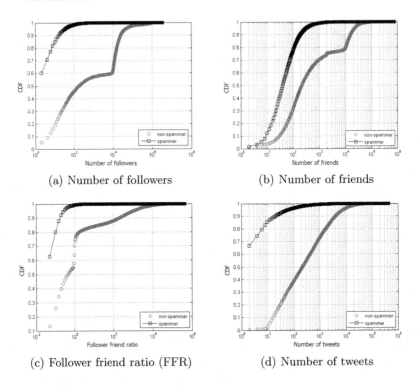

(a) Number of followers   (b) Number of friends

(c) Follower friend ratio (FFR)   (d) Number of tweets

Fig. 1. Cumulative distribution function of content attributes

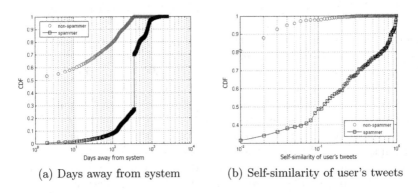

(a) Days away from system   (b) Self-similarity of user's tweets

Fig. 2. Cumulative distribution function of content attributes

to say, spammers are more likely to post similar or duplicate tweets than non-spammers.

Content attributes and behavior attributes of spammers and non-spammers are different from each other, those attributes are useful to distinguish spammers from non-spammers. In general, the analysis of those attributes show that there is a probability to detect spammers based on content attributes and behavior attributes. Next, we describe our method to detect spammers based on logistic regression model.

3.3 Classifier Based on Logistic Regression Model

Logistic regression model is a classifier that focus on the binary classification problem in which result can take on only two values, 0 and 1 [10]. So we can build a spammer classifier for online social network, then inputs are some features of a user, and output maybe 1 if it is a spammer user, or 0 otherwise. 0 is also called negative class, and 1 is called positive class. The ABLR method is based on this model. Logistic regression is based on a hypothesis function $h_\theta(x)$, which is

$$h_\theta(x) = \frac{1}{1 + e^{-\theta^T x}} \qquad (1)$$

Equation 1 is called logistic function or sigmoid function. $x = (x_1, x_2, ..., x_n)$ is a n-dimensional vector, which represents content attributes and behavior attributes of a user in social network. $\theta = (\theta_1, \theta_2, ..., \theta_n)$ is also a n-dimensional vector, which represents the corresponding parameters to x. We make the following definition, $x = (x_1, x_2, ..., x_n)$ is a attributes vector of user u, then if $h_\theta(x) = 0$ means u is a non-spammer, else $h_\theta(x) = 1$ means u is a spammer. Obviously, $h_\theta(x) \in \{0, 1\}$, which exactly corresponds with the need. Given the logistic regression model and training data, next step we need to do is finding the fittest θ for the model. A well known method is fit the parameters via maximum likelihood. For logistic regression model, the cost function $J(\theta)$ is

$$J(\theta) = \frac{1}{m} \sum_{i=1}^{m} Cost(h_\theta(x^i), y^i) \qquad (2)$$

$$Cost(h_\theta(x), y) = \begin{cases} -\log(h_\theta(x)) & if\ y = 1 \\ -\log(1 - h_\theta(x)) & if\ y = 0 \end{cases} \qquad (3)$$

Then we can use labeled data to train the model, the problem is transferred to find the optimum parameter vector $\theta = (\theta_1, \theta_2, ..., \theta_n)$ to minimize cost function $J(\theta)$. Gradient descent method is a kind of appropriate method to solve the problem of finding the optimum parameter to minimization. The method is described as Algorithm 1. Firstly, we set a suitable initial parameter vector θ_0, threshold ε, max iteration steps M and learning rate α empirically. Then if it does not meet threshold requirement or does not reach the max step M, the iteration continues. By this method, we will find a local optimal solution. We can alter the initial parameter vector θ_0, and get the global optimal solution finally.

We can obtain spammer classifier according to Eq. 1 after getting global optimal parameter $\hat{\theta}$. Given a user's attributes, that classifier is used to predict whether the user is a spammer or not.

Algorithm 1. Gradient descent method for logistic regression

Input:

    Initial parameter vector $\theta_0 = (\theta_1, \theta_2, ..., \theta_n)$;

    Threshold ε

    The max iteration step M

    The learning rate α

Output:

    Optimum parameter vector $\hat{\theta} = (\hat{\theta}_1, \hat{\theta}_2, ..., \hat{\theta}_n)$

  1: Calculate the initial cost function $J(\theta_0)$;

  2: Set $\theta = \theta_0$;

  3: **while** $(|J(\hat{\theta}) - J(\theta)| \geq \varepsilon)$ and $(step \leq M)$ **do**

  4:     update θ, $\theta = \hat{\theta}$;

  5:     $\hat{\theta}_j = \hat{\theta}_j - \alpha \frac{\partial}{\partial \theta_j} J(\theta_j)$;

  6:     step = step + 1;

  7: **end while**

  8: return $\hat{\theta}$;

---

4   Experiments and Analysis

In this section, we verify the spammer detection approach by several metrics in Sect. 4.1. In order to adequately estimate the performance of spammer detection method, precision, recall, F_1, AUC-ROC and AUC-PR are included in evaluation metrics. In Sect. 4.2, our spammer detection method is compared with several existing methods and some analyses are made subsequently.

4.1   Evaluation Metrics

In this section, to access the effectiveness and efficiency of proposed ABLR method, we use standard information retrieval metrics of precision, recall, F_1 value, AUC-ROC and AUC-PR. The precision (p) of a class X represents the ratio of the number of users classified correctly to the total predicted as users of class X. The recall (r) of a class X is the ratio of the number of users classified correctly to the total number of class X. There is a matrix to explain precision and recall [15], illustrated in Table 2.

Table 2. Matrix to explain precision and recall

		Predicted	
		Spammer	Non-spammer
True	Spammer	a	b
	Non-spammer	c	d

Each value in the matrix represents the number of elements in their original class and how they are predicted. In Table 2, the precision(p_{spam}) and the recall(r_{spam}) of class spammer are calculated as $p_{spam} = a/(a + c)$ and $r_{spam} = a/(a + b)$. The F_1 metric is related to precision and recall, and is defined as $F_1 = 2pr/(p + r)$. Another metric to evaluate the performance is receiver operating characteristic (ROC), or ROC curve, which is a graphical plot that illustrates the performance of a binary classifier system as its discrimination threshold varies. The curve is created by plotting the true positive rate against the false positive rate at various threshold settings. $AUC - ROC$ is the area under the curve, which is equal to the probability that a classifier will rank a randomly chosen positive instance higher than a randomly chosen negative one. $AUC - PR$ is area under the precision-recall curve, which has properties much like the convex hull in ROC space [7].

4.2   Result and Comparasion

The spammer detection experiments are set up in a machine with Intel 2.40 GHz dual core and 8.00 GB memories. The compile environment is JDK 1.7 and MAT-LAB R2013a. The classification experiments are performed using a 5-fold cross-validation. In each test, the original sample is partitioned into 5 sub-samples, in which 4 are used as training data and the remaining one is used as test data. This process is repeated 5 times, with each of 5 sub-samples used exactly once as test data, thus producing 5 results (Fig. 3).

Table 3. Result of spammer detection

	Dataset1	Dataset2	Dataset3	Dataset4	Dataset5
p_{spam}	0.9243	0.9196	0.9292	0.9217	0.9432
r_{spam}	0.9145	0.8882	0.9131	0.9470	0.9502
F_1	0.9194	0.9036	0.9211	0.9342	0.9467
$AUC - PR$	0.9113	0.8869	0.9103	0.9427	0.9551
$AUC - ROC$	0.8943	0.8807	0.8918	0.9175	0.9307

In Table 3, evaluation metrics are shown in different datasets. Approximately, the p_{spam} value is around 0.9, that is to say 90 percents of spammers are correctly classified, only a small fraction of non-spammers are improperly classified into spammer category. The r_{spam} value is around 0.9 in 5 sub samples, which means about 90 percents of non-spammers are identified, only 10 percents of non-spammers are not found. The F_1 values in 5 sub-samples are above 0.9, that means the classifier performs well both in precision and recall metrics. The AUC-PR is the area under curve of precision-recall, which depicts the precision and recall pairs in different situations. The AUC-ROC is the area under the curve of true positive rate against false positive rate in different thresholds. The AUC-PR and AUC-ROC values are around 0.9 in each sub-samples, which verify the effectiveness of the method.

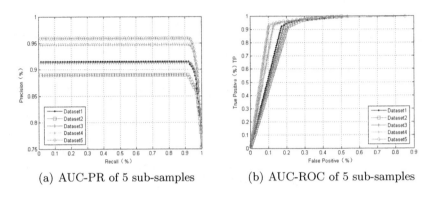

(a) AUC-PR of 5 sub-samples   (b) AUC-ROC of 5 sub-samples

Fig. 3. Curve metrics results of 5 sub-samples

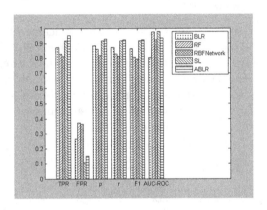

Fig. 4. Metrics comparison with existing methods

In order to verify ABLR method, several existing methods are compared with ABLR method in 6 metrics. Bayesian Logistic Regression method (BLR)[9], Random Forest method (RF)[3], RBF Network method [18], Simple Logistic method (SL)[17] are compared with ABLR method in True Positive Rate (TPR), False Positive Rate (FPR), precision (p), recall (r), F_1 and AUC-ROC metrics. In Fig. 4, ABLR gets the highest TPR in 5 methods which means ABLR performs best in classifying spammers into correct category. FPR represents classifying non-spammers into spammer category, ABLR performs better than BLR, RF and RBFNetwork, and has a similar performance to SL. That is to say, ABLR has a lower probability to classify a non-spammer into spammer category. From the third bar to the fifth bar, ABLR gets a higher score than other methods in precision, recall and F_1 metrics. In the last bar, ABLR get an AUC-ROC value exceeding 0.9, that means ABLR method performs well in different thresholds. Through the comparison experiments with other classifier, ABLR approach is verified in several metrics. Results demonstrate the effectiveness and efficiency of ABLR method in spammer detection.

5   Conclusion and Future Work

Social spammers are tricky and change their strategies continually to deceive social network system. To solve this problem, a method considering both content attributes and behavior attributes based on logistic regression. A training dataset is built up through crawling from twitter API. Several attributes are taken into account by analyzing cumulative distribution function of labeled datasets. Those attributes that can separate spammers from non-spammers are used to establish our classifier. Experimental results show that our proposed method is effective and efficient comparing with existing social spammer detecting method.

This work suggests some interesting orientation for future work. Due to the dynamic patterns of social spammers, it is important to discover attributes separating spammers from non-spammers automatically. We can further investigate methods to improve performance of the proposed model by adding online learning algorithm.

References

1. Benevenuto, F., Magno, G., Rodrigues, T., Almeida, V.: Detecting spammers on twitter. In: Collaboration, Electronic Messaging, Anti-abuse and Spam Conference (CEAS), vol. 6, p. 12 (2010)
2. Benevenuto, F., Rodrigues, T., Almeida, V.A., Almeida, J., Gonçalves, M., Ross, K.: Video pollution on the web. First Monday **15**(4), 1–20 (2010)
3. Breiman, L.: Random forests. Mach. Learn. **45**(1), 5–32 (2001)
4. Calais, P., Pires, D.E., Neto, D.O.G., Meira Jr., W., Hoepers, C., Steding-Jessen, K.: A campaign-based characterization of spamming strategies. In: CEAS (2008)
5. Chen, C., Wu, K., Srinivasan, V., Zhang, X.: Battling the internet water army: Detection of hidden paid posters. In: Proceedings of the 2013 IEEE/ACM International Conference on Advances in Social Networks Analysis and Mining, pp. 116–120. ACM (2013)
6. Chu, Z., Gianvecchio, S., Wang, H., Jajodia, S.: Who is tweeting on twitter: human, bot, or cyborg? In: Proceedings of the 26th Annual Computer Security Applications Conference, pp. 21–30. ACM (2010)
7. Davis, J., Goadrich, M.: The relationship between precision-recall and ROC curves. In: Proceedings of the 23rd International Conference on Machine Learning, pp. 233–240. ACM (2006)
8. Fetterly, D., Manasse, M., Najork, M.: Spam, damn spam, and statistics: Using statistical analysis to locate spam web pages. In: Proceedings of the 7th International Workshop on the Web and Databases: colocated with ACM SIGMOD/PODS 2004, pp. 1–6. ACM (2004)
9. Genkin, A., Lewis, D.D., Madigan, D.: Large-scale bayesian logistic regression for text categorization. Technometrics **49**(3), 291–304 (2007)
10. Hosmer, D.W., Lemeshow, S., Sturdivant, R.X.: Introduction to the logistic regression model. Wiley Online Library (2000)
11. Hu, X., Tang, J., Liu, H.: Online social spammer detection. In: Twenty-Eighth AAAI Conference on Artificial Intelligence (2014)
12. Islam, M.S., Mahmud, A.A., Islam, M.R.: Machine learning approaches for modeling spammer behavior. In: Cheng, P.-J., Kan, M.-Y., Lam, W., Nakov, P. (eds.) AIRS 2010. LNCS, vol. 6458, pp. 251–260. Springer, Heidelberg (2010)

13. Kwak, H., Lee, C., Park, H., Moon, S.: What is twitter, a social network or a news media? In: Proceedings of the 19th International Conference on World Wide Web, pp. 591–600. ACM (2010)
14. Pal, A., Counts, S.: Identifying topical authorities in microblogs. In: Proceedings of the Fourth ACM International Conference on Web Search and Data Mining, pp. 45–54. ACM (2011)
15. Ron, K., Foster, P.: Special issue on applications of machine learning and the knowledge discovery process. J. Mach. Learn. **30**, 271–274 (1998)
16. Sadowski, C., Levin, G.: Simhash: Hash-based similarity detection. Technical report, Google (2007)
17. Sumner, M., Frank, E., Hall, M.: Speeding up logistic model tree induction. In: Jorge, A.M., Torgo, L., Brazdil, P.B., Camacho, R., Gama, J. (eds.) PKDD 2005. LNCS (LNAI), vol. 3721, pp. 675–683. Springer, Heidelberg (2005)
18. Yun, Z., Quan, Z., Caixin, S., Shaolan, L., Yuming, L., Yang, S.: RBF neural network and ANFIS-based short-term load forecasting approach in real-time price environment. IEEE Trans. Power Syst. **23**(3), 853–858 (2008)

Personalized Mention Probabilistic Ranking – Recommendation on Mention Behavior of Heterogeneous Social Network

Quanle Li[✉], Dandan Song, Lejian Liao, and Li Liu

Beijing Institute of Technology, Beijing, China
le@bit.edu.cn

Abstract. Selecting a suitable person to mention on the Micro-blogging network, expressed as "@username", is a new aspect of recommendation system which carries great importance to promote user experience and information propagation. We comprehend information propagation as the reach, vitality, and effectiveness of tweet messages. In this case, we consider this mention recommendation as a probabilistic problem and propose our method named Personalized Mention Probabilistic Ranking to find out who has the maximal capability and possibility to help tweet diffusion by utilizing probabilistic factor graph model in the heterogeneous social network. A wide range of features are extracted and highlighted in our model, such as tag similarity, text similarity, social influence, interaction history and named entities. Experimental results show that our approach outperforms the state-of-art algorithms.

1 Introduction

Micro-bloggings, like Twitter and Weibo, have been widely popular and influential platforms for information diffusion and social interactions. People would like to mention their friends or celebrities to promote products, report new events, share opinions or bring up questions. Consequently, it is more valuable for any content generator, including advertisers, media workers, and common people to mention some proper users in a specific tweet, since an appropriate mention could increase their exposure, optimize new feeds, promote their reputation, accelerate information spreading and initiate public discussion cascade [1].

Liu et al. [4] observed that Twitter has become more conversational and is seeing an increasing adoption of mentions. And they claimed the most climax case witnessed that users apply @ function in over 50 percentage of tweets one day. It is the rise of mention behavior that becomes a more significant manifestation of Twitter evolution. However, even though some users realize how much difference it makes with the attention on carefulness of mentioning usernames, they are not able to find a proper candidate to mention in a short time and hence probably lose some business potential opportunities, career favorable suggestion or blasting news spread. Therefore, it is indispensable and beneficial to give a high priority to get with the mention recommendation.

© Springer International Publishing Switzerland 2015
X. Xiao and Z. Zhang (Eds.): WAIM 2015, LNCS 9391, pp. 41–52, 2015.
DOI: 10.1007/978-3-319-23531-8_4

On mention recommendation, Beidou [6] use the SVR algorithm to recommend candidates with higher relevance, which is quantified as the followers amount of the candidates. However, due to the fact that the relevant function as followers amount remains unchanged for different tweet messages, the candidates has the same result position corresponding to various queries, which raises prejudice problem. Furthermore, mentioning some users who is unwilling to response doesn't help expand the information diffusion, even though they may have considerable follower numbers. Consequently, mentioning those candidates with huge number of followers merely promises the potential scale of information diffusion but doesn't promise diffusion actual reach, vitality and effectiveness. In other words, it only guarantees they have higher potential capability to expand diffusion but doesn't guarantee they have the higher possibility to interact (reply or retweet). For instance, if we mention someone who has the maximum capability to spread tweet message but has tiny little possibility to take actions to response, the mentioned one would not be the suited person worthy of our recommendation for it practically provides no fuels for message diffusion.

We analysis the mention recommendation problem as a probabilistic problem. In the mention social network, there are different nodes with heterogeneous features including user nodes and tweet topic nodes. Specifically, user nodes is represented by their social status, social content and social relationship while tweet nodes is expressed as the tweet words as well as tweet topic. The whole mention network is assumed as a probability network while every candidate carries a different probability to be mentioned. When it comes to probability network, we introduce the factor graph theory into the mention problem because factor graph is a sophisticated and effective method.

In our work, we treat this recommend @ users recommendation system as Personalized Mentioning Probabilistic Ranking (PMPR) system. Whether a candidate should be mention or not is measured as a probability value while candidates are accounted as nodes and mentioned link considered as edges of the probabilistic network. Experiments show our method is able to fulfill the mention recommendation.

As far as we know, we are the first one to associate the mention recommendation with a probabilistic network while we also consider both the maximum capability and maximum probability of candidate's help to expand information propagation in this @ recommendation problem.

2   Related Work

Lots of technologies have been developed in recommender systems, and generally we could categorize these various systems into two main branches: content-base recommendation and collaborative recommendation. As its core, content-based recommendation is based on the availability of item descriptions and a profile that assigns importance to these characteristics. And the essential idea of collaborative systems is to recommend the similar objects by historical similar behaviors [5].

There is lots of previous work combining social network with recommender system. Bonhard and Sasse [2] showed that the relationship between advice-seeker and recommender is extremely important, so methods of indicating social closeness and taste overlap are required. And they believed that similarity and familiarity between the user and the candidates can aid judgement and decision making. In our system, we regard the familiarity between a user and his candidates as the closeness of historical social behavior.

Factor graph model was broadly applied in social network and heterogeneous Network. Tang [3] proposed a topical factor graph to analysis the social influence and Zhang [7] proposed the partially labeled factor model in order to measure the social influence locality. In our work, we present a ranking factor graph to resolve the mention relationship in the social network.

Relatively, Wang et al. [6] take users' relation as the reachable number of followers initiated by a candidate to mention of social network. The number of followers merely predicts the range and scale of potential information diffusion without considering the probability of replying the mentioned notification. The candidates doesn't help propagation if they do not response to the mentioned notification even though they may have a big fans group. In addition, the number of attainable potential followers is invariant with the message and cannot promise the probability of interaction. In their experiment, their prediction precisions are a bit low. In contrast, in order to ensure a mention notification to raise the user's response, our system integrates optimized probability to response and maximum capability to expand information propagation. Specifically our system makes recommendations by incorporating user' social influence, user's historical interactive times and the characteristics of tweets. These three factors are important for making target specific recommendations.

3   Proposed Factor Graph Method

Our system tries to recommend some users to be mentioned in a certain tweet and the candidates should compete with each other to get nominated into the recommendation list. Thereby, users' global ranking positions are highlighted and become essential or decisive factor. Give that the ranking of each candidate essential and sensitive to the recommendation. we come up with factor graph method, which is more reasonable and effective to handle the ranking issue.

Let U and T denotes the user set and tweet set respectively. Given a tweet t ($t \in T$) of a poster u ($u \in U$), we formalize mention candidates $C(u)$ (so $C(u)$ as a mentioned candidate list consisting of followees set $Followee(u)$ and name entities $NE(t)$ occurred in t. The mention social network consists of nodes and edges while nodes stand for users and edges represent the mention relationship. Let the user mentioned network defined as $G = (V, E, T)$ where users is defined as V, mention relationship is defined as E and a specific tweet defined as T.

3.1   Features

Our features can be divided into two categories: individual features and tweet features. Individual features is measured as profile similarity, historical familiarity, user social influence, user recent activity, user recent retweet activity while the tweet features are represented as content similarity including tag similarity, profile similarity and tweets text similarity.

Individual Features

– Historical Interactive Score (HIS)
Statistically, a candidate c (where $c_i \in C(u)$) who was mentioned in the historical tweets is inclined to be mentioned again in spite of the fact that a tweet may be not related to what c focused on. Intuitively, we should exploit this general user behavior as a feature. Thus We define user u's historical interaction score with candidate c as $HIS(u, c)$. Specifically, $HIS(u, c)$ is equal to the sum of the number of tweets that u mentioning c and the number of tweets that c retweeting u.

– Social Influence (SI)
Empirically, influential users with high social status have more potential and power to promote information propagation than those with lower social status, thereby candidates with high status are supposed to have apparently higher scores. The social status of c is measured by the number of his followers.

– User Recent Activity (URA)
Generally, the more active an user is, the more likely he can see the notification and reply the mentioned message. Normally users with strong dynamic would be more enthusiastic to get involved in tweet cascades and spread. Spontaneously we measure the user activity as user recent tweet numbers as users with a high activity must post many tweets recently. It's hard to imagine that a user who barely logins the micro-blogging system recently or is reluctant to posts tweets could see the mention message or get involved into retweet tide. Thus, user recent activity is presented as the number of candidate c's recent tweets $URA(c)$.

– User Recent Retweet Activity (URRA)
Hypothetically the more enthusiastic a user is about retweeting, the more probably he would retweet the tweet involved with mention notification. Therefore, we denote user recent retweet activity $URRA(c)$ as the number of c's retweets.

Tweet Features

– Content Similarity (CS)
We believe that two users who have the same interest, same circle or same experience would like to interact mutually or mention one another. In our work, every user's tweet content is on behalf of user's interest, which consists of tags, profile and historical tweets. To measure user content similarity, we present every user's previous tweets as a simple weighted bag-of-word of terms (based on TFIDF Score) and further calculate the similarity score between the poster and every candidate by cosine similarity. Ultimately, we define the content similarity as the sum of tag similarity, profile similarity and historical tweet similarity.

- **historical tweets Similarity:** Posters and candidates are represented by terms in their tweets. All the tweets are integrated into a single document. The tweet text is a term vector with TFIDF weighting scheme of all the tweets. The similarity between a user and a poster is defined as the similarity of their tweet profiles in the term vector space.
- **tags Similarity:** Users usually are labeled by some tags, which are helpful to find out who is the same kind.
- **profile Similarity:** Users' profile information contains user's self-descriptions (like a slogan), location address, university, company, sex orientation, constellation and so on. The similarity is defined as the cosine distance of their profile information in the vector space model.

The formulas of all features are shown in Table 1.

Table 1. The formulas of features

Features	Formulas	Descriptions
HIS(u,c)	= NM(u,c) + NR(c,u)	the familiarity between u and c
NM(u,c)	= num_mention(u,c)	the number of user u's tweets @ c
NR(c,u)	= num_retweet(c,u)	the amount of c's tweets carry @u information
SI(c)	= num_followers(c)	the number of c's followers
URA(c)	= Num_recent_tweets(c)	the number of c's recent tweets
URRA(c)	= Num_recent_retweets(c)	the number of c's recent retweets
CS(t,c)	= TS(u,c) + PS(u,c) + HTS(t,all_tweets(c))	the content interest match between u and c
TS(u,c)	= Jaccard_similarity(tags(u),tags(c))	tag similarity
PS(u,c)	= cosine_similarity(profile(u),profile(c))	profile similarity
HTS(t,all_tweets(c))	= cosine_similarity(t,tweets(c))	historical tweets cosine similarity

3.2   Factor Graph Representation

In the mention recommendation, the heterogeneous network contains user nodes, tweet nodes and relationship nodes, which demands the solution should be capable of well dealing with structural information besides the traditionally text information. Given that mention recommendation basically emphasizes the capability of digging out and mining the structural relationship, we post our factor graph model, which can integrate both content features and specially structural properties of heterogeneous network.

In the mention issue, what structural properties refers to is the mention edge between every tweet and the candidates. It's worth noticing that the edge definition is essential to the factor graph model and different edge definition would raise huge different experimental results. In our work, for a certain poster u, we mainly analyse the poster's tweets with mention information. Generally, users would like to mention several persons once in one tweet in order to expand the tweet propagation. Therefore, a edge would be established between every two users mentioned by the same tweet.

For example, poster u mention user v_1, v_2, v_3 in one tweet while we should build three edges for the tweet as below:

E_1: (v_1, v_2)
E_2: (v_1, v_3)
E_3: (v_2, v_3)

In factor graph theory, we could use the nodes and edges to predict candidates' mention score of every tweet. Therefore, we aim to find out a probabilistic function to predict every candidate's score and further rank the candidates with top k candidates as recommendation:

$$f : (G; U; T) \rightarrow Y \tag{1}$$

where G denotes the whole social network, U denotes the set of posters, T denotes the set of posters' tweets and Y is a hidden vector indicating a set of candidates' mention relationship probability. Specifically, the values of Y stand for the probability of being mentioned and we return top k candidates as recommendation result.

In order to describe the mention problem within the factor graph, we draw a graph as Fig. 1 to display what its structure is and how our model work the mention problem.

As the Fig. 1 presents, the heterogeneous social network consists of tweet nodes and user nodes as well as edges. t_i reflects the tweet node that is displayed as its word information while v_1, v_2, v_3,...v_i,..., v_n is respectively corresponding to one candidate represented by his social information while the $< t_i, v_i >$ of the relationship circle indicates the relationship between the poster's tweet t_i and the user v_i. What we concern with is to find out whether v_i should be mentioned by t_i. Specifically, in the factor graph model, the pair of t_i and v_i is named as invariable nodes, the $f(.)$ is designed as a feature function describing the features between t_i and v_i while in the hidden layer y_i is hidden vector revealed the probability that t_i is about to mention v_i, and $g(.)$ is a feature function defined on a edge, which indicate the hidden relationship between edges.

More importantly, the two feature functions, $f(.)$ and $g(.)$, are essential to the whole factor graph model. Specifically, $f(.)$ is formulated as below:

$$f(y_i, X_i) = \frac{1}{Z_\alpha} exp\{\sum_{i=1}^{n} \sum_{j=1}^{d} \alpha_j f(y_i, x_{i,j})\} \tag{2}$$

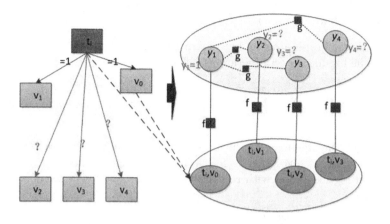

Fig. 1. Heterogeneous Factor graph model for the mention recommendation.

where $f(y_i, X_i)$ behalves the probability of y_i with features X_i, which refers to those features occurred in Subsect. 3.1. In addition, $x_{i,j}$ is one feature of a pair of invariable node, α_j represents the weight of feature function $f(.)$ and Z_α is the normalized factor.

In contrast, the edge feature function,as the correlation factor, is designed as below:

$$g(y_i, G(y_i)) = \frac{1}{Z_\beta} exp\{ \sum_{e_{i,j} \in E} \beta_{i,j} g(y_i, y_j)\} \tag{3}$$

where $g(y_i, G(y_i))$ stands for relationships between edges. Specifically factor graph theory assumes that each edge is likely to be related or subject to some specifical edges and what $g(y_i, G(y_i))$ aims at is to find out whether the relationship between one certain edge and one another happens or not. $\beta_{i,j}$ represents the weight of edge feature function $g(.)$, Z_β is the normalized factor.

In the whole factor graph, what we are mainly concerned with is to rank the probability $p(Y = 1|G)$ since $p(Y = 1|G)$ directly points out whether a mention relationship should be built or not. According to Hammersley-Cliord theory, the joint distribution of factor graph can be represented as below:

$$p(Y|G) = \prod f(y_i, X_i) g(y_i, G(y_i)) \tag{4}$$

which means for the candidate i, his being mention probability in the current tweet is defined as $p(Y|G)$ and is subject to attribute feature function and edge feature function.

Furthermore, the joint distribution can be transformed to the below formula:

$$p(Y|G) = \frac{1}{Z} exp\{ \sum_{i=1}^{n} \sum_{j=1}^{d} \alpha_j f(y_i, x_{i,j}) \sum_{e_{i,j} \in E} \beta_{i,j} g(y_i, y_j)\} \tag{5}$$

where Z is the normalized factor.

3.3   Factor Graph Model Learning

What the factor graph aims at is to learn the parameters $\theta = (\alpha, \beta)$ and here we define the log-likelihood function as below:

$$L(\theta) = log P_\theta(Y|G) = \sum_{i=1}^{n} \sum_{j=1}^{d} \alpha_j f(y_i, x_{i,j}) + \sum_{e_{i,j} \in E} \beta_{i,j} g(y_i, y_j) - log Z$$

we try to get the maximal log-likelihood function value, therefore, we apply the gradient descent algorithm to learn the θ parameter, and take the partial derivative of log-likelihood with respect to α and get the below formula:

$$\frac{\partial L(\theta)}{\partial \alpha} = \frac{\partial(\sum_{i=1}^{n} \sum_{j=1}^{d} \alpha_j f(y_i, x_{i,j}))}{\partial \theta} - \frac{\partial log Z}{\partial \theta} = E[f(y_i, x_{i,j})] - E_{Y|Y^L}[f(y_i, x_{i,j})] \tag{6}$$

However, it is difficult to solve the marginal probability and its marginal distribution from the final expression of partial derivative on α. Therefore, we introduce the sum-product algorithm to get the marginal distribution.

In addition, the way demanding the log-likelihood on the β partial derivative is same as on the α partial derivative.

3.4   Factor Graph Model Inference

With the learned parameter α and β, we can predict which has high probability to being mentioned among all the candidates in a specific tweet. The inference formula is defined as below:

$$Y = argmax_Y p(Y|G) \tag{7}$$

Y, as a hidden vector, indicates the probability for candidate to be mentioned and we select the top k candidates with top k probability.

4   Experiment Set

4.1   Data Collection

We created our training and test set by crawling data from Sina Weibo, a Twitter-like microblogging system in China provided by Sina company. We crawled every user's latest tweets, profiles, tags and the followees information. Especially, we extracted all tweets containing mention notification as our mentioned training data and testing data.

In our experiment, we collected almost 20,000 users and downloaded nearly 20,000,000 tweets that they posted. The training set and testing set shares the above data with 7:3 proportion and we applied cross-validation method into this data set.

4.2   Evaluation Measures

We introduce evaluation metrics including precision, recall, p@k, Mean Average Precision(MAP) and Normalized Discounted Cumulative Gain (NDCG) to evaluate the ranking results.

4.3   Comparison Methods

In order to compare our method with the current ranking methods, we choose several methods as our baselines:

a. Random Recommendation (RR). In this method, all the candidates are randomly chose from the followee list.
b. Influence-based Recommendation (IBR). In this algorithm, candidates will be recommended by ranking their social status, which is explicitly measured by the number of followers. The higher social status a candidate has, the bigger recommended preference he gets.
c. Content-based Recommendation (CR) This method calculates similarity between a specific tweet and followee's content information. Concretely, followee content information consists of his tweets and his profile. Here a tweet q of a user u is viewed as a query, followees' content information as document set D and the tweets from each followee i of u is considered as a document d_i. Then we calculate the similarity between q and d_i, rank the followees by their similarity value and return top k candidates.
d. Collaborative Filter Recommendation(CF) Every tweet is treated as an item, the mentioned username in every tweet is regarded as an user. Given a new tweet t of user u with mention information, we define u's followee set as Γ. For every followee j in F, we define j's whole tweets as d_j. Firstly we calculate the similarity between t and each tweet of u's historical tweets with mention notification, secondly the similarity between t and candidate c is the average value of similarity of q and the other tweets including mentioning c name. For a user u, the similarity between t and candidate c is defined as:

$$CF(t,c) = \frac{\sum\limits_{i=1}^{n} sim(t, tweet_i) * isContained(tweet_i, c)}{count(c, tweets)} \qquad (8)$$

where $tweets$ is user u's tweets set only with mention message, $tweet_i$ expresses the ith of $tweets$, i is the index of $tweets$, n represents the number of $tweets$, $count(c, tweets)$ means the number of tweets with mentioning candidate c, $sim(t, tweet_i)$ reveals the similarity between tweet t and $tweet_i$ and $isContained(tweet_i, c)$ refers to whether c is in the $tweet_i$ mentioned names list. If $tweet_i$ contains c as a mentioned name, then $isContained(tweet_i, c)$ value is 1, otherwise it's 0.

Eventually, for a tweet t we sort every candidate by his collaborative filter score and return top k candidates.

e. Whom-To-Mention method (WTM) This method is proposed by Beidou et al. [6] and mainly use a pointwise function as ranking function – Support Vector Regression(SVR) to sort the candiates' ranking positions. SVR is one traditional way to predict ranking problem in the IR fields and here is used to predict the candidates scores ordered by their relevance, which is defined as the number of each candidate's coverage of information diffusion.

5   Results and Analysis

5.1   Algorithm Performance Evaluation

From Fig. 2, we can see that our approach (PMPR) obviously makes a huge difference to information propagation for tweets.

As what the experimental result shows, Random Recommendation (RR) hardly works for this mention recommendation subject and it almost hits the bottom in all metrics due to its unstability and isolation to much information. For another, Influence-based Recommendation only shows slight effect to choose appropriate users to enhance information diffusion mostly because not all influential users have intimate bonds with the poster or show interest to the topic of the tweet. On the other hand, the performance of WTM methods doesn't look good because it is subject to its oversimple relevance defined as the number of followers' followers as well as its negligence on considering users replying possibility. The unsatisfied result of WTM expresses that only considering the range of tweet circulation may make a little contribution to information diffusion but doesn't help too much.

In addition, CR doesn't work well for this recommendation task with metric performance basically not over 0.2. The reason of the CR's performance lies in the fact that it ignores the capability, scale and range of information diffusion and social familiarity between the poster and candidates. With precision, recall and MAP performance better than the previous comparison algorithms, CF effectively promotes information diffusion of this @ problem thanks to its exploitation of logical and reasonable recommendation scheme.

$PMPR$ takes the ahead position compared to other models, which is thanks to the high accuracy of probability model. What Fig. 2 reveals also demonstrates precision, recall, F1 and MAP of $PMPR$ looks higher than 0.6 while remarkably precision of $PMPR$ is higher more 50 % than CF and NDCG of $PMPR$ fulfills 80 % increasing compared to CF.

5.2   Feature Importance Evaluation

The superiority and predominance on recommendation performance of our method was evidently attributed to the five major components of features: content similarity, history interactive score, social influence and user recent activity as well as user recent retweet activity. To analyze how each component contribute to information propagation, we conducted several contrast experiment

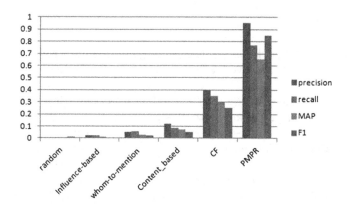

Fig. 2. Performance comparison among different algorithms in terms of precision, recall and MAP metrics.

on our method by means of removing one of these components once. Table 2 displays the affect of each component to the recommendation performance.

When our method eliminating social influence component, precision goes with 3 % drop and NDCG falls with a 13 % decline. Without content similarity as one feature, precision suffers from nearly 5 % loss and NDCG witnesses a 10 % decrease. On the other hand, the performance of precision, recall, MAP and NDCG seems insensitive to eliminating the user recent activity or user recent retweet activity, which indicates that user activity doesn't make contribute to this problem in this way.

Removing the history interactive score feature, NCDG experiences nearly 50 % decline and MAP tolerates 30 % fall. This result shows that historical interactive score takes up the most crucial place and plays a dominant role in the recommendation for people usually like to mention the old users who were mentioned before.

In a word, features such as historical interactive score, social influence and content similarity all apparently play significant parts in this recommendation. Especially, the features, historical interactive score and name entities recognition, offer significant help to expand information diffusion in an explicit way.

Table 2. Comparison on contribution of different features components to recommendation performance

Features	all	NO_HIS	NO_SI	NO_CS	NO_URA	NO_URRA
precision	0.729208	0.4848	0.60148	0.675	0.71723	0.72356
recall	0.833256	0.7036	0.80363	0.7435	0.823715	0.81391
MAP	0.6436	0.42001	0.52804	0.53419	0.60133	0.6092
NDCG	0.58571	0.3324	0.5253	0.553	0.580532	0.57402

6   Conclusion

We propose a novel model, named as Personalized Mention Probabilistic Ranking, to help users deal with overwhelmed information to find appropriate candidates to mention.

we consider the mention recommendation as a probabilistic ranking problem and apply the factor graph model to this issue. With mention relationship as edges and candidates as nodes, we establish the $PMPR$ model to fit the problem,then learning the relative parameter and inference the final recommendation users. Experiments show the $PMPR$ model is better than all the compared algorithms so far. We conducted extensive experiments on a real data set crawled from Sina Weibo. Given our experiment data set, we showed that users mutual interactive history vouches for high-quality of users to help information diffusion while the content similarity enhanced the high-relevance of the tweet and candidates. Besides, our analysis also revealed that the exploitation of users social influence allows for constructing broader information coverage.

References

1. Predicting Responses to Microblog Posts. In: Proceedings of the 2012 Conference of the North American Chapter of the Association for Computational Linguistics: Human Language Technologies. Association for Computational Linguistics (2012)
2. Bonhard, P., Sasse, M.A.: 'knowing me, knowing you' - using profiles and social networking to improve recommender systems. BT Technol. J. **24**(3), 84–98 (2006)
3. Wang, C., Yang, Z., Tang, J., Sun, J.: Social influence analysis in large-scale networks. In: Proceedings of the 15th ACM SIGKDD Conference on Knowledge Discovery and Data Mining (2009)
4. Liu, Y., Kliman-Silver, C., Mislove, A.: The tweets they are a-changin': Evolution of Twitter users and behavior. In: Proceedings of the 8th International AAAI Conference on Weblogs and Social Media (ICWSM'14), Ann Arbor, MI, June 2014
5. Pazos-Arias, J.J., Vilas, A.F., Daz Redondo, R.P.: Recommender systems for the social web (2012)
6. Wang, B., Wang, C., Bu, J., Chen, C., Zhang, W.V., Cai, D., He, X.: Whom to mention: expand the diffusion of tweets by @ recommendation on micro-blogging systems. In: Schwabe, D., Almeida, V.A.F., Glaser, H., Baeza-Yates, R.A., Moon, S.B. (eds.) WWW, pp. 1331–1340. International World Wide Web Conferences Steering Committee/ACM (2013)
7. Zhang, J., Liu, B., Tang, J., Chen, T., Li, J.: Social influence locality for modeling retweeting behaviors

A Novel Recommendation Algorithm Based on Heterogeneous Information Network Similarity and Preference Diffusion

Bangzuo Zhang$^{(\boxtimes)}$, Shulin Tang, Zongming Ying, Yongjian Cai, Guiping Xu, and Kun Xu

School of Computer Science and Information Technology,
Northeast Normal University, Changchun 130117, China
{zhangbz, tangsl388, yinzm953, caiyj374,
xugp940, xuk357}@nenu.edu.cn

Abstract. Recommender system has been proposed as a key tool to overcome the problem of information overload. In the present era of big data, how to utilization the side information of users, items is a new challenge. This paper put forward a novel solution based on the heterogeneous information network and preference diffusion. The similarity matrices of users and items are initially computed based on meta-path similarity algorithm; three new preference diffusion methods has been proposed to fuse the similarity matrix and the user-item rating matrix; finally uses the traditional recommendation techniques based on matrix factorization to predict the results. With the experiment in a classical data set MovieLens 100 K and the movie attributes extended from IMDb, verifies the effectiveness of the solution that with heterogeneous information network to make full use of users and item attributes information and the preference diffusion with rating matrix can improve the recommendation accuracy effectively.

Keywords: Heterogeneous information network · Matrix factorization · Meta-path · Collaborative filtering · Recommender system

1 Introduction

Recommender system [1] has been proposed as a key tool to overcome the problem of information overload [2]. Now, recommender systems are ubiquitous online, when you rent movies on Netflix, buy products from Amazon, or perform myriad other tasks online, recommender systems make suggestions based on your past behavior.

Collaborative filtering (CF) [3] is the most successful and widely used recommendation technique. The basic idea of the system is that if users shared the same interests in the past, they will also have similar tastes in the future. CF techniques are often classified as being either memory-based or model-based. The traditional user-based or item-based technique is said to be memory-based because the original rating database is held in memory and used directly for generating the recommendations. In model-based approaches, on the other hand, the raw data are first processed offline, as described for item based filtering or some dimensionality reduction techniques. At run time, only the "learned" model is required to make predictions.

X. Xiao and Z. Zhang (Eds.): WAIM 2015, LNCS 9391, pp. 53–64, 2015.
DOI: 10.1007/978-3-319-23531-8_5

The Netflix Prize competition, which was completed in 2009, showed that advanced matrix factorization methods, can be particularly helpful to improve the predictive accuracy [4].

In the past few decades, significant progress has been made in recommender system performance by deploying CF to exploit user-item relations, which are typically encoded in a user-item rating matrix. However, in recent years, a large number of recommendation scenarios have emerged in which various additional information sources are available [5]. There are two types of additional information that is considered useful for improving the recommendations: rich side information about users and items, and information about the situation in which users interact with items. In such cases, CF can be either enhanced to improve recommendation performance further or else be utilized to pursue different tasks other than product/item recommendation [6].

Heterogeneous information network (HIN) [7], a novel big data mining tools, provides a opportunity to use more information from the attributes of the users and items. It is a new recommendation scenario that offers promising new information that goes beyond the user-item rating matrix. In the real world movie recommendation scenarios, people who like a movie, he/she may not only see the rating scores from other users, and also take into account the attributes of the film, such as the actor and the director. The film studio also deliberately uses these attributes as a main selling point. Therefore, the attributes of users and movies must be taken into account and it is an opportunity for more accurate recommendation.

Recommender system based on heterogeneous information network is still in its infancy. The existed methods usually only considered the heterogeneous information network formed by the interaction between users and items, and gave up the user-item rating information, which is the main important source for the collaborative filtering system. So, how to fusion the information of heterogeneous information network and the user-item rating matrix is a novel challenge.

This paper use the heterogeneous information networks to model the relation between users and items in a recommender system to leverage the semantic meaning of the types of nodes and links in a network, and propose a novel recommendation algorithm that can exploit such rich semantics and solve real-world problems. The most important work in this paper is to fuse the similarity matrix based on the meta-path of the heterogeneous information network and the user-item rating matrix by three methods. The experiment in the MovieLens 100 K verifies the effectiveness of the proposed solution. The contributions of this paper are summarized as below.

1. It proposes a new framework of fusion the recommender system based on the heterogeneous information networks and the traditional CF technique.
2. Two similarity computing methods based on the meta-path in the heterogeneous information network have been compared.
3. It first suggested three preference diffusion methods to fuse the user/item similarity matrix with user-item rating matrix, which captured the subtle similarity semantics among peer objects in the networks.
4. The experiments based on two famous matrix factorization methods, SVD and NMF, demonstrated the effectiveness of the proposed method.

2   Related Works

Heterogeneous information network [7], also called multi-relational social network [8], is originated from the real world that is an interconnected world, most of data or informational objects are interconnected or interact with each other, forming numerous, interconnected, and sophisticated networks, such interconnected networks are called information networks. Given a set of entities types $A = \{A\}$ and a set of relations type $R = \{R\}$, formally, information network can be defined as follows.

Definition 1 (Information Network). An information network is defined as a directed graph $G = (V, E)$ with an object type mapping function $\tau: V \rightarrow A$ and a link type mapping function $\varphi: E \rightarrow R$, where each object $v \in V$ belongs to one particular object type $\tau(v) \in A$, each link $e \in E$ belongs to a particular relation $\varphi(e) \in R$.

Examples of information networks include social networks, the World Wide Web, research publication networks, and so on. Clearly, information networks are ubiquitous and form a critical component of modern information infrastructure. Different from the traditional network definition, definition 1 explicitly distinguish object types and relationship types in the network. When the types of objects $|A| > 1$ or the types of relations $|R| > 1$, the network is called heterogeneous information network [7–11], otherwise, it is a homogeneous information network.

If a relation exists from type A to type B, denoted as $A R B$, A and B are the source type and target type of relation R, which is denoted as $R.S$ and $R.T$, respectively. The inverse relation R^{-1} holds naturally for $B R^{-1} A$. According to [9–11], the concept of network schema is defined to describe the meta structure of a network.

Definition 2 (Network Schema). The network schema, denoted as $TG = (A, R)$, is a meta template for a heterogeneous network $G = (V, E)$ with the object type mapping τ: $V \rightarrow A$ and the link mapping $\varphi: E \rightarrow R$, which is a directed graph defined over object types A, with edges as relations from R.

The star network [9] is a specific heterogeneous information network, sometimes constructed from relation set, such as records in a relational database, with each tuple in the relation as the center object and all attribute entities linking to the center object.

Definition 3 (Star Network). An information network, $G = (V, E)$ with $T + 1$ types of objects (i.e., $V = \{X_t\}_{t=0}^{T}$), if $\forall e = <x_i, x_j> \in E$, $x_i \in x_0 \wedge x_j \in x_t(t \neq 0)$, or vice versa, is called with star network schema. G is then called a star network. Type x_0 is the center type (called the target type) and types $x_t(t \neq 0)$ are attribute types.

In the heterogeneous information network, two objects can be connected through different attributes, these different attributes path represents a different meaning, and the relatedness of objects depends on the search path in the networks. The meta search path is defined as meta-path [9] (also called relevance path [19, 20]).

Definition 4 (Meta-path). A meta-path P is a path defined on the graph of network schema $TG = (A, R)$, and is denoted in the form of $A_1 \xrightarrow{R_1} A_2 \xrightarrow{R_2} \ldots \xrightarrow{R_l} A_{l+1}$, which defines a composite relation $R = R_1 \circ R_2 \circ \ldots \circ R_l$ between types A_1 and A_{l+1}, where "$\circ$" denotes the composition operator on relations.

Thus, a typed, semi-structured heterogeneous network captures essential semantics of the real world. It turns out that this level of abstraction has great power in not only representing and storing the essential information about the real world, but also providing a useful tool to mining knowledge from it, by exploring the power of links. It provides an opportunity and challenge for recommender system to fuse more information of users and items.

The VideoLectures.net (http://videolectures.net/), one of the world's largest academic video hosting Web portals [10], is the first time that heterogeneous information network has been taken into account the methodology where all the structural contexts and the text documents are fused together. HeteRecom [11], a prototype system architecture which published in KDD 2012, is the first work of direct using heterogeneous information network for recommendation. OptRank [12] modeled a social tagging system as a heterogeneous information network to alleviate the cold start problem like users' tagging behaviors, social networks, tag semantics and item profiles. HeteroMF [13], which published in WWW 2013, take into account that users can be engaged in interactions with multiple types of entities across different contexts, leading to multiple rating matrices, that is, user can have interactions in a heterogeneous information network. Liu et al. [14] propose a novel heterogeneous information network approach to host innovative citation information.

The work that most like to ours is that did by Yu et al. [15–17]. They put forward a novel framework [15, 16], using meta-path based latent features to represent the connectivity between users and items, and then defining a recommendation model with such latent features and use Bayesian ranking optimization techniques to estimate the model. The drawback is that they take the user-item rating matrix as the implicit user feedback, and change the matrix to binary, so they can't make full use of the rating scores. There has an embarrassing condition that traditional collaborative filtering recommender system only uses the user-item rating matrix and the recommender system based on the heterogeneous information network only use the link information of user and item. For recommendation evaluation, measures like root mean square error (RMSE) and mean absolute error (MAE) are the standard evaluation metric, but they use top-10 mean reciprocal rank (MRR) metrics in information retrieval, so their work can't compare with the others.

3   The Proposed Method

This Section proposed a novel solution to fuse the heterogeneous information network and the traditional collaborative filtering recommender method. Through established the heterogeneous information network on the user and item attributes, to compute the similarity matrix of user and item based on meta-path similarity algorithm, and puts forward three preference diffusion methods to fuse the user-item rating matrix, finally uses the traditional matrix factorization techniques to predict.

For a recommender system, with n users and m items, the denotation defined as follows. $US = \{U_1, U_2, \ldots, U_n\}$, U_i is a user; $WS = \{I_1, I_2, \ldots, I_m\}$, I_i is an item; $UA = \{UA_1, UA_2, \ldots, UA_k\}$, UA_i is an attribute of a user, k is the number of user attributes; $IA = \{IA_1, IA_2, \ldots, IA_t\}$, IA_i is an attribute of an item, t is the number of item attributes; $UW \in R^{n*m}$, is the matrix after fused, with n rows and m columns.

3.1 Similarity Computing Based on Meta-Path

Similarity search has been extensively studied for traditional categorical and numerical data types in relational data. There are also a few studies leveraging link information in networks. Most of these studies are focused on homogeneous networks or bipartite networks, such as personalized PageRank [21] (P-PageRank), SimRank [22]. However, these similarity measures are disregarding the subtlety of different types among objects and links. Adoption of such measures to heterogeneous networks has significant drawbacks: the objects of different types and links carry different semantic meanings, and it does not make sense to mix them to measure the similarity without distinguishing their semantics. To distinguish the semantics among paths connecting two objects, until now there are two similarity framework based on the meta-path in a heterogeneous information network, PathSim [18] and HeteSim [19, 20].

PathSim is a similarity measure on the symmetric meta-path. The intuition is that two similar peer objects should not only be strongly connected, but also share comparable visibility. Given a symmetric meta-path $P(A_1A_2\ldots A_i\ldots A_{l+1})$, the PathSim between two object s and t ($s \in R_1.S$ and $t \in R_l.T$) can be computed as Eq. (1).

$$PathSim(s,t) = \frac{2 \times |\{p_{s \to t} : p_{s \to t} \in P\}|}{|\{p_{s \to s} : p_{s \to s} \in P\}| + |\{p_{t \to t} : p_{t \to t} \in P\}|} \tag{1}$$

Where $p_{s \to t}$, $p_{s \to s}$ and $p_{t \to t}$ are a path instance between s and t, s and s, and t and t, respectively. Obviously, round trip meta-paths with the form of $P = P_1 P_1^{-1}$ are always symmetric.

HeteSim has two properties, one is a uniform measure, which can measure the relatedness of objects with the same or different types in a uniform framework, the other is a path-constrained measure, the relatedness of object pairs are defined based on the search path that connects two objects through following a sequence of node types. Similarly, HeteSim can also be computed as Eq. (2).

$$HeteSim(s,t|R_1 \circ R_2 \circ \ldots R_l) = \frac{1}{|O(s|R_1)||I(t|R_l)|} \sum_{i=1}^{|O(s|R_1)|} \sum_{j=1}^{|I(t|R_l)|} HeteSim(O_i(s|R_1), I_j(t|R_l)|R_2 \circ \ldots R_{l-1})$$

$$\tag{2}$$

Where $O(s|R_1)$ is the out-neighbors of s based on relation R_1, and $I(t|R_l)$ is the in-neighbors of t based on relation R_l. When s may not have any out-neighbors or t may not have any in-neighbors following the meta-path, their similarity value to be 0. Equation (2) shows that computing $HeteSim(s, t|P)$, must to iterate over all pairs $O_i(s|R_1)$, $I_j(t|R_l)$ of (s, t) along the meta-path (s along the path, while t against the path), and collect the relatedness of these pairs.

For a star schema network, the meta-paths are always even-length, maybe symmetric, and we do not need some trick on decomposition the meta-path [20]. So the meta-path P can be divided into two equal-length path P_L and P_R. For a relation $A \xrightarrow{R} B$, W_{AB} is an adjacent matrix between type A and B. U_{AB} is a normalized matrix of W_{AB} along the row vector,

$$HeteSim(A_1, A_{l+1}|P) = HeteSim(A_1, A_{l+1}|P_L P_R) = U_{P_L} U'_{P_R^{-1}} \qquad (3)$$

So the HeteSim can be normalized as Eq. (4),

$$NHS(s, t|P) = \frac{U_{P_L}(s, :) U'_{P_R^{-1}}(t, :)}{\sqrt{\|U_{P_L}(s, :)\| \|U'_{P_R^{-1}}(t, :)\|}} \qquad (4)$$

PathSim and Normalization of HeteSim (NHS) both obey the properties of non-negativity, identity of indiscernible, and symmetry, so they are both a semi-metric measure. The difference between them is that NHS can evaluate the heterogeneous objects based on arbitrary path, while PathSim can only evaluate similarity of same typed objects based on a symmetric path.

Given a meta-path, these two similarity metrics can compute a similarity score, such as two movies, can explore follow the meta-path from this movie to the actors, then to another movie, the process can repeat several times, that is,

movie-(actor-movie)^r;

r is a natural number, the bigger r will get a longer meta-path. Since the similarity is less than or equal to 1, the value will decay quickly, so actually r only need to get a small number. Similarly, the similarity between users can also be computed with the user attribute. Note that meta-path usually have multiple, so the similarity computing can consider multiple attributes, which also accords with the really intuition.

For each user meta-path P_i, such as user-gender-user, which means that the users with same gender maybe have the same taste to watch similar movies, so get the user similarity matrix $USM(UA_i) \in R^{n*n}(0 < i \leq k)$; and for each item meta-path P_j, such as movie-director-movie, which means the movies has the same director maybe has the same genre, therefore can also get the item similarity matrix $ISM(IA_i) \in R^{m*m}(0 < i \leq t)$. Denote L as the number of meta-path, L similarity matrix can be generated based on the specific meta-path. Considering that different similarity semantics could have different importance to recommended, the fused similarity for users U_i, U_j can be defined as follows,

$$sim(U_i, U_j) = \frac{1}{L} \sum PathSim(U_i, U_j) \; or \; sim(U_i, U_j) = \frac{1}{L} \sum HeteSim(U_i, U_j) \qquad (5)$$

Similarly, the fused similarity for items I_i, I_j can also be defined as follows,

$$sim(I_i, I_j) = \frac{1}{L} \sum PathSim(I_i, I_j) \; or \; sim(I_i, I_j) = \frac{1}{L} \sum HeteSim(I_i, I_j) \qquad (6)$$

3.2   User and Item Preference Diffusion Methods

To alleviate the data sparsity challenge faced by the traditional CF techniques and improve the recommendation accuracy, how to fuse the similarity and the rating information is a big question. The similarity between users with PathSim and HeteSim indicates the rich user preference, while the similarity between items discovered the rich information between items.

For a collaborative filtering recommendation system, which has n users and m items, the user-item rating matrix must be a matrix with n rows and m columns. Considering the user similarity matrix is a square matrix of n rows and n columns, and the item similarity matrix is a square matrix of m rows and m columns. Inspiring by work of Yu et al., we put forward three preference diffusion methods by matrix multiplication as follows.

- Method 1: (user-item rating matrix) × (item similarity matrix)
- Method 2: (user similarity matrix) × (user-item rating matrix)
- Method 3: (user similarity matrix) × (user-item rating matrix) × (item similarity matrix)

After the preference diffusion process, we can get the matrix UW for recommendation in the next step.

The preference diffusion process for method 3 with a toy example demonstrates in Fig. 1, and the new matrix isn't sparse as before.

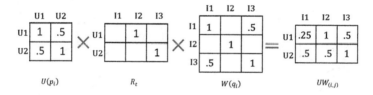

Fig. 1. preference diffusion process for method 3 with a toy example

3.3   Recommendation with Matrix Factorization

Matrix factorization method is often classified as the model-based collaborative filtering technology. The Netflix competition shows that it's very effective. The traditional matrix factorization method always use the user-item rating matrix, and our method proposed to use the matrix UW after the process of preference diffusion. Two most famous matrix factorization technologies have been used.

- Singular value decomposition (SVD) [23], factorizes the matrix into a product of two low rank matrices (user-profile and item-profile) to estimate the missing entries.
- Non-negative matrix factorization (NMF) [24], the difference is that it constrain the low rank matrices forming the factorization to have non-negative entries.

If using the one way breadth first search, the computation complexity for similarity based on the meta-path is $O(n * m * L)$, if using bidirectional search it is $O(n^3)$.

The preference diffusion method uses the matrix multiplication is $O(n^3)$, so the complexity is $O(n^3)$. Two prediction methods using matrix factorization, the complexity is close the same, both $O(n^3)$. So, the complexity of the whole algorithm is $O(n^3)$, the proposed method do not increase the global time complexity.

4   Experiments

4.1   The Data Set and the Network Schema

The experiments use the popular MovieLens 100 K data set collected by the Group-Lens Research Project at the University of Minnesota (http://grouplens.org/datasets/movielens/). The data set contains 100,000 ratings (1−5) from 943 users on 1682 movies. In order to provide more information of the movie attributes, we extended the dataset from the corresponding movies in Internet Movie Database (IMDb). For the convenience of the evaluation and repeating the experimental results, we use the users and movies data set that has been divided and enclosed in the MovieLens 100 k data set (U1 to U5).

The network schema for the users and the movies are both belong to star networks, and shown in Figs. 2 and 3, respectively. The edges in the graph are bidirectional, so don't mark the directions.

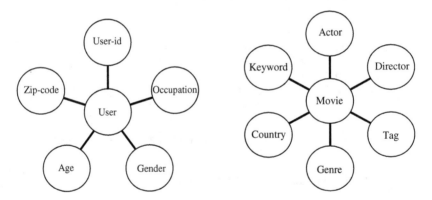

Fig. 2. The users network schema   Fig. 3. The movies network schema

4.2   Experimental Setup

The evaluation metric is Mean Absolute Error (MAE), which is the deviation from the true value in the test data set. The smaller the MAE is, the more accurate the results are.

For computing the similarity matrix based on the meta-path in the heterogeneous information network, since PathSim required a symmetric meta-path, the length of meta-path only can be set to 2 (r = 1). Noted that for HeteSim (Normalization of HeteSim), which is same as PathSim if set r = 1, so in these experiments the length of meta-path is set to 4 (r = 2). Of course, for Hetesim, the length of meta-path can be set longer, but it will take more time and run slower.

For the user and item preference diffusion methods, we use the three methods, denote as M = 1, or 2, or 3 respectively.

4.3 Experimental Results and Analysis

In order to verify the effective of our proposed methods, we gives 2 different similarity computing methods, as well as 3 preference diffusion methods, based on 2 recommendation technologies based on matrix factorization, SVD and NMF, the results is given in Figs. 4 and 5, respectively.

In Fig. 4, SVD has been used as a collaborative filtering recommendation algorithm, the MAE values with HeteSim similarity method is significantly smaller than the Path-Sim method, achieved remarkable effect of recommendations. Because the symmetric meta-path required by PathSim constrained the length of meta-path only can be set to 2, while HeteSim don't need this constrain, the length can be longer (set to 4). So the longer the length of meta-path is, the better the recommendation quality. The preference diffusion methods can also effectively affect the recommendation results, noted that items information is richer than users' information, and preference diffusion by fusion item similarity matrix is better than fusion user similarity matrix, at the same time, fusion of user and item similarity matrix is better than only fusion item similarity matrix. Although use the PathSim similarity method, the results of fusion user similarity matrix and item similarity matrix and only fusion with item are very close, but in HeteSim method (meta-path length set to 4), the MAE values is lower than the other two kinds of preference diffusion methods, which indicates fusion of more information is superior.

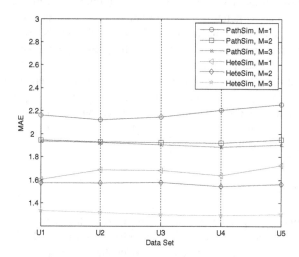

Fig. 4. Results based on SVD for 2 similarity methods with 3 preference diffusion methods

In Fig. 5, the recommendation algorithm use NMF, we can see more obvious results consistent with Fig. 4, that is, the longer the meta-path length is, the better the prediction results. From the preference diffusion methods, the fusion of item similarity

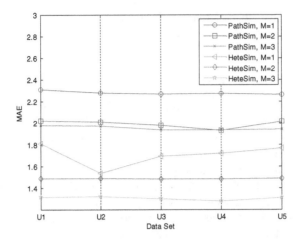

Fig. 5. Results based on NMF for 2 similarity methods with 3 preference diffusion methods

matrix is better than fusion user similarity matrix, although the results in the U4 data set has a unexpected anomaly, but from the view of the average effect, the former is obviously better than that of the latter.

Comprehensive analysis from Figs. 4 and 5, we found that use of SVD and NMF, MAE value has not much difference, so we will consider more matrix factorization method, test them with different similarity computing methods and different preference diffusion methods, it's one of our future works. We can also find that the MAE values of preference diffusion method 2 and 3 are close, and these two methods both use the movies similarity matrix, it has very important relation with our data set expansion approach, which is introduced in Subsect. 4.1. Due to the number of user attributes is significantly less than the movie attributes, so the preference diffusion with the item similarity matrix will greatly affect the results, so that the effect is not obvious for both fusion the item similarity matrix and the user similarity matrix method. This also gives us an inspiration, for better recommendation results, we need pay more attention to mine more user and item attributes, and select the reasonable meta-path length, which are our possible future works, too. We will also consider larger data sets to further validate the proposed method.

5   Conclusions

In this era of big data, people pay more attention to the network structure of the relationship between data. The heterogeneous information network is a favorable tool to mine the big data, and an opportunity and challenge to study the recommender system. By establishing the heterogeneous information network based on the user and item attributes in the recommender system, we introduce 2 similarity computing methods, then use 3 preference diffusion methods based on the matrix multiply to fuse with user-item rating matrix, finally use the classical collaborative filtering techniques based on matrix factorization to predict the results. The purposed method is verified in the international standard data sets, MovieLens 100 K, and extends the movie attributes from IMDb data set. Therefore, the use of heterogeneous information network to introduce more information from the attributes of user and item and with preference diffusion methods can effectively use the internal information of data, and can improve the accuracy of recommendation.

Acknowledgments. This work is supported by Jilin Provincial Science and Technology Key Project (20150204040GX), National Training Programs of Innovation and Entrepreneurship for Undergraduates (201410200042).

References

1. Lu, L., Medo, M., Yeung, C.H., Zhang, Y.-C., Zhang, Z.-K., Zhou, T.: Recommender systems. Phys. Rep. **519**(1), 1–49 (2012)
2. Speier, C., Valacich, J.S., Vessey, I.: The influence of task interruption on individual decision making: an information overload perspective. Decis. Sci. **30**(2), 337–360 (1999)
3. Goldberg, D., Nichols, D., Oki, B.M., Terry, D.: Using collaborative filtering to weave an information tapestry. Commun. ACM **35**(12), 61–70 (1992)
4. Jannach, D., Zanker, M., Felfernig, A., Friedrich, G.: Recommender Systems: An Introduction. Cambridge University Press, Cambridge (2011)
5. Adomavicius, G., Tuzhilin, A.: Toward the next generation of recommender systems: A survey of the state-of-the-art and possible extensions. IEEE Trans. Know. Data Eng. **17**(6), 734–749 (2005)
6. Shi, Y., Larson, M., Hanjalic, A.: Collaborative Filtering beyond the User-Item Matrix: A Survey of the State of the Art and Future Challenges. ACM Computing Surveys (CSUR) **47**(1), Article No.3 (2014)
7. Han, J.: Mining Heterogeneous Information Networks by Exploring the Power of Links. In: Gama, J., Costa, V.S., Jorge, A.M., Brazdil, P.B. (eds.) DS 2009. LNCS, vol. 5808, pp. 13–30. Springer, Heidelberg (2009)
8. Cai, D., Shao, Z., He, X., Yan, X., Han, J.: Community mining from multi-relational networks. In: Jorge, A.M., Torgo, L., Brazdil, P.B., Camacho, R., Gama, J. (eds.) PKDD 2005. LNCS (LNAI), vol. 3721, pp. 445–452. Springer, Heidelberg (2005)
9. Sun, Y., Han, J.: Mining Heterogeneous Information Networks: Principles and Methodologies. Morgan & Claypool, Beijing (2012)
10. Grčar, M., Lavrač, N.: A methodology for mining document-enriched heterogeneous information networks. In: Elomaa, T., Hollmén, J., Mannila, H. (eds.) DS 2011. LNCS, vol. 6926, pp. 107–121. Springer, Heidelberg (2011)
11. Shi, C., Zhou, C., Kong, X., Yu, P., Liu, G.: HeteRecom: a semantic recommendation system in heterogeneous networks. In: Proceedings of the 18st ACM SIGKDD Conference on Knowledge Discovery and Data Mining, pp. 1552–1555 (2012)
12. Feng, W., Wang, J.: Incorporating heterogeneous information for personalized tag recommendation in social tagging systems. In: Proceedings of the 18th ACM SIGKDD International Conference on Knowledge Discovery and Data Mining, pp. 1276–1284 (2012)
13. Jamali, M., Lakshmanan, L.: HeteroMF: recommendation in heterogeneous information networks using context dependent factor models. In: Proceedings of the 22nd International Conference on World Wide Web, pp. 643–654 (2013)

14. Liu, X., Yu, Y., Guo, C., Sun, Y., Gao, L.: Full-text based context-rich heterogeneous network mining approach for citation recommendation. In: ACM/IEEE Joint Conference on Digital Libraries (JCDL 2014), London (2014)
15. Yu, X., Ren, X., Sun, Y., Sturt, B., Khandelwal, U., Gu, Q., Norick, B., Han, J.: Recommendation in heterogeneous information networks with implicit user feedback. In: Proceedings of 2013 ACM International Conference Series on Recommendation Systems (2013)
16. Yu, X., Ren, X., Sun, Y., Gu, Q., Sturt, B., Khandelwal, U., Norick, B., Han, J.: Personalized entity recommendation: a heterogeneous information network approach. In: Proceedings of 2014 ACM International Conference on Web Search and Data Mining (WSDM 2014) (2014)
17. Yu, X., Ren, X., Gu, Q., Sun, Y., Han, J.: Collaborative filtering with entity similarity regularization in heterogeneous information networks. In: Proceedings of IJCAI-2013 HINA Workshop (2013)
18. Sun, Y., Han, J., Yan, X., Yu, P.S., Tianyi, W.: PathSim: meta path-based top-K similarity search in heterogeneous information networks. PVLDB 4(11), 992–1003 (2011)
19. Shi, C., Kong, X., Yu, P.S., Xie, S., Wu, B.: Relevance search in heterogeneous networks. In: Proceedings of the 15th International Conference on Extending Database Technology, pp. 180–191 (2012)
20. Shi, C., Kong, X., Huang, Y., Yu, P.S., Bin, W.: HeteSim: a general framework for relevance measure in heterogeneous networks. IEEE Trans. Knowl. Data Eng. 26(10), 2479–2492 (2014)
21. Page, L., Brin, S., Motwani, R., Winograd, T.: The pagerank citation ranking: bringing order to the web. Technical report, Stanford Univ. Database Group (1998)
22. Jeh, G., Widom, J.: Simrank: a measure of structural-context similarity. In: Proceedings of the Eighth ACM SIGKDD International Conference on Knowledge Discovery and Data Mining (KDD), pp. 538–543 (2002)
23. Sarwar, B.M., Karypis, G., Konstan, J.A., Reidl, J.: Application of dimensionality reduction in recommender system - a case study. In: ACM WebKDD 2000 Web Mining for E-Commerce Workshop (2000)
24. Lee, D.D., Seung, H.S.: Learning the parts of Objects by Non-negative Matrix Factorization. Lett. Nat. 401, 788–791 (1999)

Information Diffusion in Online Social Networks: Models, Methods and Applications

Changjun Hu[1], Wenwen Xu[1(✉)], and Peng Shi[2]

[1] School of Computer and Communication Engineering,
University of Science and Technology Beijing,
Beijing 100083, China
xuwenwen.ustb@163.com
[2] National Center for Materials Service Safety,
University of Science and Technology Beijing,
Beijing 100083, China

Abstract. Online social networks are now recognized as an important platform for the spread of information, based on their convenient usage and strong interaction. The research on information diffusion in online social networks is valuable in both theoretical and practical perspective. In this paper, we present a survey of representative methods dealing with information diffusion. First, we analyze the main factors related to diffusion. Second, we propose a taxonomy that summarizes the state-of-the-art based on the type of insight provided to the analyst. We discuss various existing methods that fall in these broad categories and analyze their strengths and weaknesses. Finally, to facilitate future work, a discussion of incorporating dynamic properties of networks, diffusing in heterogeneous networks, and a life-cycle model of information diffusion is provided.

Keywords: Online social networks · Information diffusion models · Network structure · Social crowds

1 Introduction

With the development of Web 2.0 techniques and popularity of smart devices, social networks, such as forums, blogs, and micro-blogging, continue to expand its role in the social ecosystem, establishing itself as a powerful platform for distributing content and consuming information. Users in social networks can share, discuss and forward various kinds of information – ranging from personal daily events to important and global event related information – in real-time. It's easy to know when and where a piece of information propagated after observation, but not how did it diffuse. The study on information diffusion can facilitate our understanding of social phenomenon and provide some insights regarding the complex structure, human dynamics and social system.

The study of information diffusion initially started out as a subject of biology and sociology. Studies related to deterministic models for infectious diseases go as far back as the early 20th century. In 1927, Kermack and McKendrick proposed the SIR model

© Springer International Publishing Switzerland 2015
X. Xiao and Z. Zhang (Eds.): WAIM 2015, LNCS 9391, pp. 65–76, 2015.
DOI: 10.1007/978-3-319-23531-8_6

in which they considered a mixed population with only three compartments: susceptible, infective and removal [6]. They used those compartments to depict the dynamics in epidemiology. It was subsequently modified into the SIS model which incorporated the concept of repeated infections [7]. In social sciences, Rogers [8] synthesized research from over 508 diffusion studies and developed a theory applied to the adoption of innovations among individuals and organizations in 1962. In 1944, Paul Lazarsfeld et al. [9] presented their findings drawn from the scientific study of small groups that mass media information was channeled to the masses through opinion leaders. Empirical studies of diffusion were desirable, but historically had suffered from some difficulties. Most of observational studies were short-term from small-scale networks, and data on diffusion was limited.

The prevalence of online social networks has brought new opportunities and challenges for the study of information diffusion. On one hand, massive data generated by online social networks provides an important resource for researchers. Unlike offline communication, online exchange is convenient and carried by all ages regardless of geographical location. With billions of connections, individuals constitute a large-scale network. Services like Twitter, Facebook and Digg offer a wide diversity in user profiles and record the message posting/replying time stamp of each user through the embedded timeline. Messages are shared and updated frequently in these sites. Based on these features, researchers justify and extend the earlier hypothesis and theoretical models, and also observe many interesting phenomena. However, online social networks are large-scale and interactions between people are complex, making the traditional methods inefficient in this area. On the other hand, there have lots of application scenarios related to information diffusion in online social networks, such as recommendation system, marketing and so on. Be able to quantify and measure the diffusion of information can greatly improve performances in these scenarios.

A variety of methods have been attempted in order to capture the diffusion process in online social networks, ranging from thermodynamics to epidemiology to probabilistic generative and statistical inference. These methods differ from each other with respect to conditions for use, model complexity, and prediction performance. It's essential to analyze and summarize existing works to form a clear and comprehensive understanding to this meaningful research area.

In this paper, we present a survey of representative methods dealing with information diffusion. The key to modeling the diffusion is to understand crucial factors associated with the spread process. So we star from the factors that affect online information diffusion. These factors provide a variety of aspects to analyze. Then, we classify the extant methods to provide a simplified view of this field.

The rest of this paper is organized as follows: Sect. 2 analyzes the composition of online social networks, and discusses the main factors related to information diffusion. In Sect. 3, we provide a taxonomy that summarizes existing diffusion models, based on the type of insight provided to the analyst, such as structural, staged and feature-based. For each class, we analyze representative methods, point out their strengths and weaknesses. We conclude and propose some future work in Sect. 4.

2   Factors Related to Information Diffusion

An online social network can be described as a system that connected users permit to communicate and share information. Based on relationships, such as friendships, memberships, common interest or prestige, individuals connect with others to form complex structure. Due to this structure, the connected individuals gather with a large number of ongoing events. They influence each other by interactions to form a variety of networking crowds, explicitly or implicitly. Based on relational structure and social networking crowds, various kinds of information have been quickly published and diffused [4]. Therefore, structure of online social networks provides a base platform and social crowds directly promote information diffusion.

2.1   Network Structure

A social network is a structure made up of a set of social actors and a set of ties between these actors. There is a widespread intuitive sense that the spreading process is differently in different types of online social networks. For example, forums and blogs mainly diffuse information in a one-to-many or point-to-plane way. After a publisher releases messages, who will read and what action he/she will take are both unknown. Instant messaging services like MSN, Skype use point-to-point communications methodology. User can initiate a chat session with a particular individual whenever someone on his/her private list is online. While micro-blogging allows network members control of the designated recipient to a certain extent (e.g., "someone-only", "selected friends", "all friends" or "everyone" in Twitter) [12].

In fact, a variety of communication mechanisms are the result of different social ties between nodes. Social ties refer to the links that connect individuals with others. The strength of a tie is a combination of the amount of time, the emotional intensity, the intimacy, and the reciprocal services which characterize the tie [10]. It's usually defined as the relative overlap of the neighborhood of two nodes in the network. Strong ties are responsible for decision making and knowledge generation [2, 14]. Weak ties are often characterized by less frequent communication and tend to exist between dissimilar others, so they offer access to diverse pools of novel information and are more valuable than strong ties for dissemination [1, 10, 13]. The theory of weak ties and strong ties serves as a basis for contemporary information diffusion theories.

2.2   Social Crowds

At some degree, behavioral characteristics of users have an effect on information diffusion. Naaman et al. [15] conducted an analysis of the content of messages posted by individuals. Wu et al. [17] performed an analysis by examining which and what percentage of Twitter users were information generators and information consumers. Java et al. [16] provided many descriptive statistics about Twitter users, and found that the main types of user intentions were: daily chatter, conversations, sharing information and reporting news. Furthermore, users play different roles of information source, friends or information seeker in different communities. In general, information sources are individuals like celebrities, representatives of media outlets and other formal organizations that have a much larger number of followers than their followees. If a post is published by an information source, it will trigger larger cascade and wider spread. The concept of centrality can be used to quantify the relative importance of an individual. Network scientists have invented dozens of centrality measures, such as closeness centrality, betweenness centrality, eigenvector centrality and so on. Individuals with high centrality scores are often more likely to be key conduits of information, and early adopters of anything that spreads in a network.

Individuals form networking crowds by connecting with others. Compared with traditional dissemination, information diffusion in online social networks is among crowds with strong interactions. Specially, group sentiment has a significant impact on the diffusion process. Thelwall et al. [18] used SentiStrength algorithm [19] to analyze the 30 largest spiking events in Twitter posts over a month. The results showed that popular events were normally associated with increases in negative sentiment strength, and peaks of interest in some events had stronger positive sentiment than the time before the peak.

2.3   Information

Information in social networks reflects users' online activities, and plays an indispensable role in diffusion analysis.

Thelwall et al. [20] assessed the volume of blogger postings that news stories of different types. They believed that this would reveal the topics that bloggers interested in. Romero et al. [21] found that hashtags of different topics exhibited different mechanics of spread. Hashtags on politically controversial topics were particularly persistent, with repeated exposures continuing to have unusually large marginal effects on adoption. In addition, traditional empirical studies and models of diffusion only consider a single contagion propagating through the social network, independent of any other contagion [23]. While these models have been effective, they do not capture the effects of multiple contagions cascading through the network simultaneously. It's essential to extend the present understanding of information diffusion combined with information characteristics.

3   Models of Diffusion

Diffusion models can not only visualize the spread process, but also infer the possible paths and predict trend, providing theoretical basis and technical support for application based information diffusion. We can classify diffusion models in three main groups: structural models, staged models, and feature models, depending on the type of insight provided to the analyst. In the following, we will detail these categories and analyze some representative efforts in them.

3.1   Structural Models

The structural models are based on the assumption that interactions at microscopic level between pairs of users and the topology of their interconnections can explain the dynamics of the spreading process at the macroscopic level [32]. A social network is represented by a directed graph, where nodes are users and edges are relationships. Each node is either active (an adopter of information) or inactive. The state of nodes can transform from inactive to active, but not in the opposite direction.

3.1.1   Methods

There are two fundamental models in this category, namely Independent Cascades Model (IC) [24, 25] and Linear Threshold Model (LT) [26]. These two models focus on different diffusion aspects. IC model is sender-centered, and requires a diffusion probability to be associated to each edge. The newly activated nodes try once to influence their inactive neighbors independently with diffusion probabilities assigned to links. While LT model is receiver-centered, and requires an influence degree to be defined on each edge and an influence threshold for each node. An inactive node is influenced by its active neighbors if the sum of their weights exceeds the threshold for the node. In both cases, the process ends when no more activation happens.

In IC and LT propagation models, the diffusion process proceeds iteratively in a synchronous way along a discrete time-axis, starting from a set of initially activated nodes [5]. However, in the real world, information diffuses along the continuous time axis, and time-delays can occur during the propagation asynchronously [29]. A substantial research effort has been dedicated to solving this problem. Saito et al. [29, 30] extended IC and LT models to incorporate asynchronous time delay, namely asynchronous independent cascades (AsIC) and asynchronous linear threshold (AsLT). By using a continuous time-axis and time-delay parameter on each edge, the asynchronous versions can treat the time delay of each node independently. Guille et al. [32] proposed a concrete model relied on the AsIC to predict the temporal dynamics of diffusion. Three dimensions (semantic, social, and time) are considered in the model. And they used the machine learning techniques to infer diffusion probabilities between nodes of the network (Fig. 1).

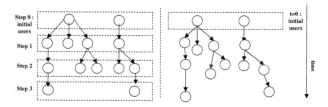

Fig. 1. Comparison of a cascade modeled by IC (left) and AsIC (right)

In addition, Song et al. [28] proposed an information flow model to leverage interpersonal diffusion rate based on Continuous-Time Markov Chain. Ho et al. [33] designed two models: a rigid-propagation relationship model and a loose-propagation relationship model. Based on above models, they defined two kinds of influence trees to estimate information diffusion. Game theory had also been applied to diffusion study. Zinoviev et al. [34, 35] used game theory to study information flow in a star-like network with one sender and N receivers, based on the psychological traits of the participants.

3.1.2   Applications

The structural models extract the structure of online social networks and leverage the interplay between pairs of users to present diffusion, so the process can be associated with the topological properties, such as scale, range, and temporal properties. These models are usually applied to predict the diffusion paths, study the cascading behavior and provide personalized recommendation. The information flow model [28] was used to predict who would most quickly receive the information during a certain time period. Galuba et al. [31] focused on characterizing the propagation of URLs. Based on LT model, they constructed a propagation model that predicted which users were likely to mention which URLs.

However, there are some limitations in this category. First, from the perspective of time, the topology researchers obtained is static, corresponding to a snapshot of the original network. This structure records all observed relationships before being collected. For example, links established long ago and links created recently are collected at the same time. Second, the weight on edges is either constant or drawn from distributions, which means the influence of user satisfies certain probability function. This method can't effectively quantify the strength of a tie. Moreover, the structural models assume that people can only be influenced by their neighbors of the network, ignoring external effects. In the real scenario, information reaches us through connections in social networks, as well as through the influence out-of-network sources, like newspapers, TV stations and online news sites [22].

3.2   Staged Models

Extracting the structure of network is a grand challenge. In many scenarios, the network over which diffusion takes place is implicit or even unknown. Consequently, some studies focus on a different aspect of propagation: states. The information adoption process can be divided into several states, and staged models investigate the flow of information based on switching among these states.

3.2.1   Methods

Most of the current efforts in this category widely reuse those of epidemiology as a basis to tackle the propagation [32]. The underlying hypothesis is that the information diffusion is analogous to the spread of infective disease. Applying to diffusion scenario, the Susceptible-Infected-Removal (SIR) model can be described as follows. Initially, all nodes are susceptible the corresponding individuals do not know the message that is being propagated, and then partly become "infected" by learning it. At each time step, the infectious nodes try to infect the susceptible nodes with probability or enter the recovered stage. Infecting a node means passing the new message to that node or influencing the node's attitude toward something. Recovered stage means becoming immune. The recovered nodes cannot further diffuse information.

Combining the inherent evolutionary mechanism in online social networks, considerable studies have been devoted to refining the epidemic models. Abdullah et al. [36] extended the SIR model to investigate news spreading on Twitter. They allowed the entry of a new susceptible similar to the birth rate in traditional epidemiology as tweets from infectious individuals reached to their followers' stream causing the population size to grow. Xiong et al. [37] proposed the Susceptible- Contacted-Infected- Refractory (SCIR) model, with two absorbing states: the infected state and the refractory state. Susceptible agents might be infected by spreaders or enter the contacted state in which agents had read the topic but had not yet made a retweeting decision. Contacted agents still had opportunities to spread the topic, but they might lose interests and become refractory. Analytical results demonstrated that even if very few infected agents came forth during the evolution, there were a number of agents that had read the information, implying they were actually influenced.

However, the epidemic methods focus on change of states, without distinguishing individual's capability to diffuse information. User's propagation ability is not evenly distributed between all nodes, so it is necessary to develop more complex model that take into account this characteristic.

Based on the assumption that diffusion of information was governed by the influence of individual nodes, Yang et al. [38] developed a Linear Influence Model (LIM). The influence functions were presented in a non-parametric way and could be estimated using a simple least squares procedure. Experiments showed that LIM outperforms classical time series forecasting methods when predicting the magnitude and rate of information diffusion. Bakshy et al. [39] examined the interplay of social networks and social influence in the adoption of online content. They found that the content being diffused through social influence tended to have more limited audience (Fig. 2).

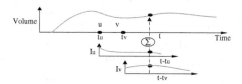

Fig. 2. Linear influence model

3.2.2 Applications

The staged models are interested in the dynamics of the process and focus on the repartition of the population of nodes into several states. Epidemic models are widely applied to study diffusion of information such as opinions and rumors. Simulation results showed that the modified model can effectively emulate the trend spreading dynamics on Twitter for a range of events [36]. Epidemic models are also adopted to deal with the problem that locating the source of a spreading process [40, 41]. Influence based models can be helpful for several areas such as marketing, expert location, and advertisement. Marketers, planners and other change agents could benefit by adopting more precise metrics of influence [3].

There are still some limitations in this category. Epidemic models attempt to describe and explain what happens on the average at a large scale population. However, many topics propagate without becoming epidemics or involve small population, where epidemic models would be inappropriate. Influence based models need more data and many simulations to yield a useful prediction. The number of users in online social networks is enormous. Specially, users have different influence in different aspects. The question how to quantify the influence of users is still a big challenge.

3.3   Feature Models

Online content exhibits some features such as temporal rhythms, multiple sources, competition contagion and so on. Feature models based on these characteristics to study dynamic patterns of information diffusion.

3.3.1   Methods

The study temporal patterns associated with online content and how the content's popularity grows and fades over time can give us an insight to the dynamics of human attention. Golder et al. [42] found that messaging in online social networks exhibited temporal rhythms. Yang et al. [43] developed the K-Spectral Centroid (K-SC) clustering algorithm to uncover the temporal dynamics of online content. However, the lack of a clear distinction between internal and external information flow in networks means that the possible functional shapes of events are all far from clear.

The information we experience comes to us continuously over time, assembled from many small pieces, and conveyed through online social networks as well as other means, like newspapers, TV stations. Crane et al. [44] analyzed time series of daily views for nearly 5 million videos on YouTube. When a time series showed an immediate and fast rise, they asserted that the rise was likely caused by external influence. Myers et al. [22] presented a probabilistic generative model of information emergence in networks, in which information could reach a node via the links of the social network (internal exposure) or through the influence of external sources (external exposure). The connection between exposures and infections was established by defining the notion of the exposure curve that mapped the number of times node U had been exposed to information I into the probability of U getting infected. Eventually, either the arrival of exposures would cease, or the node would become infected and then expose to its neighbors.

Considering the case of multiple contagions, Myers et al. [23] developed a statistical model that allowed for competition as well as cooperation of different contagions. They quantified how much exposing a user to one piece of content could increase or decrease their receptiveness to another piece of content and captured how these interactions changed with time. Besides, researchers also extended epidemic models to model multiple-meme propagation [46, 47]. Beutel et al. [46] introduced the concept of interaction factor and developed a model SI1|2S based on the SIS model. They showed that there was a phase transition: if the competition is harsher than a critical level, then winner takes all, otherwise, the weaker virus survives.

3.3.2   Applications

Feature models based on information characteristics can help us to study dynamic patterns of diffusion. The study of temporal patterns can be used to predict popularity of online content [48, 49]. Szabo and Huberman [48] found that the final popularity was reflected by the popularity in early period by investigating Digg and Youtube. Then they proposed a linear regression method to predict the long-term popularity. Considering the impact of exogenous source, Gomez et al. [45] introduced an additional node m that represented an external source. Every node u could get infected by the external source m with a very small probability. Results in [22] showed that about 71 % of the information volume in Twitter can be attributed to network diffusion, and the remaining 29 % is due to external events and factors outside the network.

There are areas for further research. Due to features like temporal dynamics, multiple sources and topic type, information itself has inherent propagation property. How to quantify this property and how to combine with user's role when diffusing? Explore these questions will facilitate us better understand the propagation mechanism.

4   Conclusion and Future Directions

In this paper, we survey representative methods dealing with information diffusion in online social networks. Based on the type of insight, existing diffusion models can be categories into three genres: structural models, staged models and feature models. For each category, we analyze representative methods, point out their strengths and weaknesses.

In spite of these encouraging results, information diffusion in online social networks still presents numerous academic and practical challenges. Hereafter we provide a discussion about possible improvements to bring.

1. Incorporating dynamic properties of networks. Most of diffusion methods rely on the assumption that the underlying network remains static, such as IC and LT. In real scenario however, networks evolve over time. It's essential to refine diffusion models to incorporate dynamic evolving nature of social networks. A better alternative to the network graph is an interaction graph [12]. Compared with the follower network, the interaction graph can reflect the actual interactions between the individuals. Besides, the impact of outside source, selecting mechanism of individual interactive object and dynamics of personal social relationships [50] should be considered when dealing with interplay between nodes.
2. Diffusing in heterogeneous networks. In the field of information diffusion, most researches assume the existence of a homogeneous network where nodes and edges are of the same type. However, in real scenario, we often have to deal with heterogeneous social networks where the nodes are of different kinds, edges are of dissimilar types [11]. Combination of different source networks and analyzing the

users' influence is helpful to understand diffusion mechanism in heterogeneous networks.

3. A life-cycle model of information diffusion. Existing researches focus on modeling spread process from one node to another, lack of comprehensive understanding of information diffusion. In fact, multiple factors contribute to information diffusion. In different phase may have different leading factor. Building a life-cycle model may better approximate the propagation in social networks.

Acknowledgement. This work was supported by the National 973 Project (No. 2013CB329605).

References

1. Taxidou, I., Fischer, P.M.: Online analysis of information diffusion in twitter. In: Proceedings of the Companion Publication of the 23rd International Conference on World Wide Web Companion, pp. 1313–1318 (2014)
2. Bakshy, E., Rosenn, I., Marlow, C., et al.: The role of social networks in information diffusion. In: Proceedings of the 21st International Conference on World Wide Web, pp. 519–528. ACM (2012)
3. Bakshy, E., Hofman, J.M., Mason, W.A., et al.: Everyone's an influencer: quantifying influence on twitter. In: Proceedings of the Fourth ACM International Conference on Web Search and Data Mining, pp. 65–74. ACM (2011)
4. Fang, B., Jia, Y., Han, Y., et al.: A survey of social network and information dissemination analysis. Chinese Science Bulletin, 1–10 (2014)
5. Guille, A., Hacid, H., Favre, C., et al.: Information diffusion in online social networks: a survey. ACM SIGMOD Rec. **42**(2), 17–28 (2013)
6. Kermack, W.O., McKendrick, A.G.: Contributions to the mathematical theory of epidemics. Proc. R. So. Lon. **115**(772), 700–721 (1927)
7. Kermack, W.O., McKendrick, A.G.: Contributions to the mathematical theory of epidemics. II. The problem of endemicity. Proc. R. Soc. Lond. Ser. A **138**(834), 55–83 (1932)
8. Rogers, E.: Diffusion of Innovations, 4th edn. Free Press, Tampa (1995)
9. Lazarsfeld, P.F., Berelson, B., Gaudet, H.: The People's Choice: How the Voter Makes up his Mind in a Presidential Campaign. Columbia University Press, New York (1965)
10. Granovetter, M.: The strength of weak ties. Am. J. Sociol. **78**(6), 1 (1973)
11. Parthasarathy, S., Ruan, Y., Satuluri, V.: Community Discovery in Social Networks: Applications, Methods and Merging Trends social Network Data Analytics, pp. 79–113. Springer, US (2011)
12. Zinoviev, D.: Social Networking and Community Behavior Modeling: Qualitative and Quantitative Measures. Information Diffusion in Social Networks, 146 (2012)
13. Ten, K.S., Haverkamp, S., Mahmood, F., et al.: Social network influences on technology acceptance: a matter of tie strength, centrality and density. In: BLED 2010 Proceedings Paper, vol. 40 (2010)
14. Zhao, J., Wu, J., Feng, X., et al.: Information propagation in online social networks: a tie-strength perspective. Knowl. Inf. Sys. **32**(3), 589–608 (2012)
15. Naaman, M., Boase, J., Lai, C.H.: Is it really about me?: message content in social awareness streams. In: Proceedings of the 2010 ACM Conference on Computer Supported Cooperative Work, pp. 189–192. ACM (2010)

16. Java, A., Song, X., Finin, T., et al.: Why we twitter: understanding microblogging usage and communities. In: Proceedings of the 9th WebKDD and 1st SNA-KDD 2007 Workshop on Web Mining and Social Network Analysis, pp. 56–65. ACM 2007
17. Wu, S., Hofman, J.M., Mason, W.A., et al.: Who says what to whom on twitter. In: Proceedings of the 20th International Conference on World Wide Web, pp. 705–714. ACM (2011)
18. Thelwall, M., Buckley, K., Paltoglou, G.: Sentiment in Twitter events. J. Am. Soc. Inf. Sci. Technol. **62**(2), 406–418 (2011)
19. Thelwall, M., Buckley, K., Paltoglou, G., et al.: Sentiment strength detection in short informal text. J. Am. Soc. Inf. Sci. Technol. **61**(12), 2544–2558 (2010)
20. Thelwall, M., Byrne, A., Goody, M.: Which types of news story attract bloggers. Inf. Res. **12**(4), 12–14 (2007)
21. Romero, D.M., Meeder, B., Kleinberg, J.: Differences in the mechanics of information diffusion across topics: idioms, political hashtags, and complex contagion on twitter. In: Proceedings of the 20th International Conference on World Wide Web, pp. 695–704. ACM (2011)
22. Myers, S.A., Zhu, C., Leskovec, J.: Information diffusion and external influence in networks. In: Proceedings of the 18th ACM SIGKDD International Conference on Knowledge Discovery and Data Mining, pp. 33–41. ACM (2012)
23. Myers, S.A., Leskovec, J.: Clash of the contagions: cooperation and competition in information diffusion. In: ICDM, vol. 12, pp. 539–548 (2012)
24. Goldenberg, J., Libai, B., Muller, E.: Talk of the network: a complex systems look at the underlying process of word-of-mouth. Mark. Lett. **12**(3), 211–223 (2001)
25. Goldenberg, J., Libai, B., Muller, E.: Using complex systems analysis to advance marketing theory development: modeling heterogeneity effects on new product growth through stochastic cellular automata. Acad. Mark. Sci. Rev. **9**(3), 1–18 (2001)
26. Granovetter, M.: Threshold models of collective behavior. Am. J. Sociol. **83**(6), 1420 (1978)
27. Gruhl, D., Guha, R., Liben-Nowell, D., et al.: Information diffusion through blogspace. In: Proceedings of the 13th International Conference on World Wide Web, pp. 491–501. ACM (2004)
28. Song, X., Chi, Y., Hino, K., et al.: Information flow modeling based on diffusion rate for prediction and ranking. In: Proceedings of the 16th International Conference on World Wide Web, pp. 191–200. ACM (2007)
29. Saito, K., Kimura, M., Ohara, K., Motoda, H.: Behavioral analyses of information diffusion models by observed data of social network. In: Chai, S.-K., Salerno, J.J., Mabry, P.L. (eds.) SBP 2010. LNCS, vol. 6007, pp. 149–158. Springer, Heidelberg (2010)
30. Saito, K., Kimura, M., Ohara, K., et al.: Selecting information diffusion models over social networks for behavioral analysis. In: Machine Learning and Knowledge Discovery in Databases, pp. 180–195. Springer, Berlin Heidelberg (2010)
31. Galuba, W., Aberer, K., Chakraborty, D., et al.: Outtweeting the twitterers-predicting information cascades in microblogs. In: Proceedings of the 3rd Conference on Online Social Networks. USENIX Association, p. 3 (2010)
32. Guille, A., Hacid, H.A: Predictive model for the temporal dynamics of information diffusion in online social networks. In: Proceedings of the 21st International Conference Companion on World Wide Web, pp. 1145–1152. ACM (2012)
33. Ho, C.T., Li, C.T., Lin, S.D.: Modeling and visualizing information propagation in a micro-blogging platform. In: 2011 International Conference on Advances in Social Networks Analysis and Mining (ASONAM), pp. 328–335. IEEE (2011)

34. Zinoviev, D., Duong, V.A.: Game theoretical approach to modeling full-duplex information dissemination. In: Proceedings of the 2010 Summer Computer Simulation Conference. Society for Computer Simulation International, pp. 358–363 (2010)

35. Zinoviev, D., Duong, V., Zhang, H.: A game theoretical approach to modeling information dissemination in social networks. arXiv preprint arXiv:1006.5493 (2010)

36. Abdullah, S., Wu, X.: An epidemic model for news spreading on twitter. In: 2011 23rd IEEE International Conference on Tools with Artificial Intelligence (ICTAI), pp. 163–169. IEEE (2011)

37. Xiong, F., Liu, Y., Zhang, Z., et al.: An information diffusion model based on retweeting mechanism for online social media. Phys. Lett. A **376**(30), 2103–2108 (2012)

38. Yang, J., Leskovec, J.: Modeling information diffusion in implicit networks. In: 2010 IEEE 10th International Conference on Data Mining (ICDM), pp. 599–608. IEEE (2010)

39. Bakshy, E., Karrer, B., Adamic L.A.: Social influence and the diffusion of user-created content. In: Proceedings of the 10th ACM Conference on Electronic Commerce, pp. 325–334. ACM (2009)

40. Lokhov, A.Y., Mézard, M., Ohta, H., et al.: Inferring the origin of an epidemic with dynamic message-passing algorithm. arXiv preprint arXiv:1303.5315 (2013)

41. Antulov-Fantulin, N., Lancic, A., Stefancic, H., et al.: Statistical inference framework for source detection of contagion processes on arbitrary network structures. arXiv preprint arXiv:1304.0018 (2013)

42. Golder, S.A., Wilkinson, D.M., Huberman, B.A.: Rhythms of social interaction: messaging within a massive online network. Communities and Technologies, pp. 41–66. Springer, London (2007)

43. Yang, J., Leskovec, J.: Patterns of temporal variation in online media. In: Proceedings of the Fourth ACM International Conference on Web Search and Data Mining, pp. 177–186. ACM (2011)

44. Crane, R., Sornette, D.: Robust dynamic classes revealed by measuring the response function of a social system. Proc. National Acad. Sci. **105**(41), 15649–15653 (2008)

45. Gomez R.M., Leskovec, J., Krause, A.: Inferring networks of diffusion and influence. In: Proceedings of the 16th ACM SIGKDD International Conference on Knowledge Discovery and Data Mining, pp. 1019–1028. ACM (2010)

46. Beutel, A., Prakash, B.A, Rosenfeld, R., et al.: Interacting viruses in networks: can both survive?. In: Proceedings of the 18th ACM SIGKDD International Conference on Knowledge Discovery and Data Mining, pp. 426–434. ACM (2012)

47. Sahneh, F.D., Scoglio, C.: May the best meme win!: new exploration of competitive epidemic spreading over arbitrary multi-layer networks. arXiv preprint arXiv:1308.4880 (2013)

48. Szabo, G., Huberman, B.A.: Predicting the popularity of online content. Commun. ACM **53** (8), 80–88 (2010)

49. Bao, P., Shen, H.W., Huang, J., et al.: Popularity prediction in microblogging network: a case study on sina weibo. In: Proceedings of the 22nd International Conference on World Wide Web Companion. International World Wide Web Conferences Steering Committee, pp. 177–178 (2013)

50. Arnaboldi, V., Conti, M., Passarella, A., et al.: Dynamics of personal social relationships in online social networks: a study on twitter. In: Proceedings of the First ACM Conference on Online Social Networks, pp. 15–26. ACM (2013)

2nd International Workshop on Human Aspects of Making Recommendations in Social Ubiquitous Networking Environments (HRSUNE 2015)

Mining Personal Interests of Microbloggers Based on Free Tags in SINA Weibo

Xiang Wang[✉], Xiang Yu, Bin Zhou, and Yan Jia

School of Computer, National University of Defense Technology,
Changsha, China
{xiangwangcn,xiangyu,zhoubin,yanjia}@nudt.edu.cn

Abstract. SINA Weibo, a micro-blogging service, provides users with an application to record their brief postings about their lives. They can tag themselves using free tags to show their personal characteristics, but 78.2 % of all users do not tag themselves. In this paper, we try to mine user's personal interests based on the self-defined free tags. A directed weighted graph is constructed with the interactive relations between users. We suppose that if two users have interacted with each other, they may share latent common interests. So interests can be propagated from a user to its interacted friends. Experiments on three SINA Weibo datasets show that our method performs better than exiting methods in mining user's personal interests. Moreover, our method is more efficient than these methods since we do not use the content of user's tweets but the user self-defined free tags only.

Keywords: Interest · Microblog · Tag · SINA Weibo

1 Introduction

SINA Weibo, which is a Chinese microblogging website like Twitter, is one of the most popular sites in China. As an emerging Web 2.0 application, it combines the short message service and social networking and attracted 503 million registered users in December 2012 to share their daily activities, interests and opinions. In SINA Weibo, information can be explosively disseminated to a large number of users. Due to its popularity and efficiency of information diffusion, large number of campaigns for business and other purposes flourish into the SINA Weibo communities. The shared content of a user indicates the user's personal interests to some extent. Users can follow their friends in real life, interested accounts like movie stars and singer stars to read what they share in their daily life. A Large number of famous persons, organizations and even general public have verified their identity. The users they follow in SINA Weibo show their interests in daily life. Because of the large number of users and potential business applications such as information recommendation, studies on mining microbloggers' interests have emerged in recent years [1–7].

Existing researches proposed many kinds of methods to mine personal interests. Some researches try to mine personal interests based on the content of the tweets users post [4, 7, 8]. Some researches try to adopt traditional keyword extraction approaches for mining personal interests [8]. A modified topic model is used to detect topic

© Springer International Publishing Switzerland 2015
X. Xiao and Z. Zhang (Eds.): WAIM 2015, LNCS 9391, pp. 79–87, 2015.
DOI: 10.1007/978-3-319-23531-8_7

interests of microbloggers based on the content of the tweets [4, 7]. As the result of topic model is hard to explain, some users try to utilize external knowledge base like Wikipedia to describe the interests of users [3, 9]. Wikipedia is useful to describe user interests because user interests can be described by the hyponymy relations of keywords/phrases due to the taxonomy of Wikipedia concepts. These methods did not utilize the rich relations between users in microblogging applications like SINA Weibo.

Tagging is an important feature of the Web 2.0 applications and helps to facilitate e.g. browsing and searching. In SINA Weibo, a user can tag itself to show its personal interests. The number of the tags is limited to no more the ten. For example, Kai-Fu Lee, who is one of the most prominent figures in the Chinese internet sector and was the founding president of Google China, labels himself with 10 tags: "IT Internet", "Innovation Works", "Venture Capital", "Education" and so on. Figure 1 shows the tags of Kai-Fu Lee to show his personal interests.

Fig. 1. Tags of Kai-Fu Lee in SINA Weibo

In this paper, we try to mine user's personal interests in SINA Weibo based on the self-defined free tags of users. We construct a directed weighted graph using the interactive relation like retweeting or notifying (@username) relations between users. If a user retweets another user's tweet or notify another user, we think they share latent common interests. Then tags for describing a user's interests can propagate to the user's friends in the interactive graph. Experiments on three SINA Weibo datasets show that our method is better than existing methods. Moreover, our method is more efficient since we do not use the content of user's tweets.

The rest of this paper is organized as follows: related works will be introduced in Sect. 2. In Sect. 3, our method based on user self-defined tags in the interactive graph will be described. Experimental results and evaluations will be provided in Sect. 4. Conclusion of this paper is made in Sect. 5.

2 Related Works

Many researches try to mine personal interests based on the content of the tweets users post. Topic model is the method to detect topics in the text content, while the detected topics indicate user's personal interests. Because of different generation ways of original tweets and retweets, He et al. [4] proposed a modified topic model to combine user original interests and retweet interests. As there are a lot of noisy tweets in SINA

Weibo such as daily chats, Xu et al. [7] introduced a latent variable to indicate whether it is related to its author's interests and modified author-topic model [10] to detect user interests. There is a problem for the results of modified topic model, which is hard to understand and use for applications such as information recommendation.

Traditional keyword extraction approaches are also introduced to mine user's personal interests [11]. Typical methods are TFIDF method and TextRank method. As there are are usually noisy and full of new words in microblogging website, Liu et al. [8] proposed a method to combine a translation-based method with a frequency-based method for keyword extraction. Keywords based methods are using keywords in the content of users to be the interests of users, but a lot of interest tags are expressed explicitly in the content of the user's tweets. For example, a person who is interested in "English Premier League", may talk about "Chelsea" or "Man Utd", but there maybe no explicit keyword of "English Premier League".

Methods using Knowledge base try to solve the problem of traditional keyword extraction approaches. These method can use the knowledge in knowledge base like Wikipedia to understand the latent semantic relations between keywords [12, 13] and find the best keyword or phrase to describe the personal interests [3]. Miao et al. [3] proposed a method to mine user interests based on the semantic graph constructed from Wikipedia. Michelson and Macskassy [14] try to discover Twitter users' personal interests by examining the entities in the content of their Tweets in Wikipedia.

3 Tag-Based Interest Mining Model

In SINA Weibo, a user can tag itself with some labels like Kai-fu Lee in Fig. 1. According to our statistical results shown in Fig. 2, we find that 78.2 % of all users do not tag themselves. In the rest 21.8 % of users, they tend to use personal tags to represent their interests and the tags they use are sparse. In this section, we first try to cluster the sparse tags with Wikipedia-based semantic relatedness methods. Then the tags spread from one user to another using label propagation algorithm to detect the interests of un-labeled and labeled users.

3.1 Clustering Tags

In SINA Weibo, although many users tag themselves, a large number of users do not tag themselves. We get 144,210,854 users from SINA Weibo API and analyze the statistical characteristics of users containing tags. We find that 78.2 % of all users in our dataset do not tag themselves. It's important to tag these users to mine their personal interests.

We also analyze the frequency of different tags and the results are shown in Fig. 2. We find that 93.84 % of user tags are not used more than 5 times, so tags in SINA Weibo are very sparse and very little tags are used by a large number of users. We remove the tags which are used less than 5 times.

There are also a lot of tags whose meanings are nearly the same. For example, someone tags computer science as "CS" while other one tags it "Computer Science".

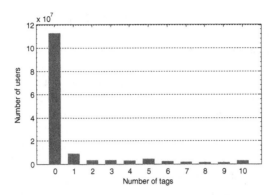

Fig. 2. Percentage of users containing different number of tags

So we have to cluster these tags together. We use a Wikipedia method named ESA [15] to compute the semantic relatedness between two tags. If the semantic relatedness between two tags is more than 0.8, we think they are in the same class. For a tag, if the semantic relatedness between a tag and any tag in a class is beyond the threshold of 0.8, we will add the tag to the class. We get 298,817 tag classes in our SINA Weibo dataset.

3.2 Tag Propagation in Interactive Graph

In SINA Weibo, a user can tag himself (or herself) with some labels. Users are connected together with following/follower relationship and some interactive relationships like retweet relationship, reply relationship and notify relationship. In this paper, we don't consider the static following/follower relationship but the interactive relationships, because the interactive relationships explicitly represent that a user influences other user. In future, static following/follower relationship will be considered. We use a weighted directed graph of users $G = (V, E, W)$ to represent relationships between users.

For a specific user u_i, there are some tags describing the characteristics. Figure 1 shows the tags of Kai-fu Lee. T_{u_i} is used to describe the set of tags for user u_i. We use $r_{u_i t_j}$ to describe the relevance score of user u_i and tag t_j, where $t_j \in T_{u_i}$. R_{u_i} is the set of relevance score of user u_i and all his (her) tags T_{u_i}. So in the interactive graph $G = (V, E, W)$, a vertex $v_i(v_i \in V)$ can be represented as $v_i = (u_i, T_{u_i}, R_{u_i})$ which show the property of user u_i.

In the interactive graph $G = (V, E, W)$, edges between two nodes are representing the retweeting or notify relation (@username). If a user u_i retweet or notify another user u_j, there is a directed edge $e_{ji}(v_j, v_i)$ from vertex v_j to vertex v_i. The weight w_{ji} of edge $e_{ji}(v_j, v_i)$ is calculated by frequency of user u_i retweet and notify u_j. We consider the retweet and notify relationships to be the same relationship. Then weight w_{ji} is calculated as Eq. (1):

$$w_{ji} = f_{ret}(u_i, u_j) \bigg/ \sum_{u_s \in retSet(u_i)} f_{ret}(u_i, u_s) \tag{1}$$

where $f_{ret}(u_i, u_j)$ is the total number of retweeting and notifying from user u_i to user u_j. $retSet(u_i)$ is the set of all users that has been retweeted or notified by user u_i. We can find that $0 \leq w_{ji} \leq 1$ from Eq. (1).

As the interactive graph is constructed between users, then label propagation algorithm can be used to spreading tags from friends to others, since we think that if two users are communicating with each other, they share latent common interests. The tags a user use in their profile show its personal interests. Then tag $t_s (t_s \in T_{u_j})$ in user u_j propagates to user u_i with weight $p_{t_s}(u_j, u_i)$, which is calculated in Eq. (2):

$$p_{t_s}(u_j, u_i) = r_{u_i t_s} \cdot w_{ji} \tag{2}$$

where $r_{u_i t_s}$ is the relevance score of user u_i and tag t_s, w_{ji} is the influence strength from user u_j to u_i in Eq. (1).

User u_i may communicate with many users and tags in these users can also probably implicit in user u_i. Then the new relevance score $r'_{u_i t_s}$ of a tag t_s to user u_i will be the sum of all users' t_s transferring to user u_i. Let $S_{Ret}(u_i)$ be the set of all users that are be retweeted or notified by user u_i, then $r'_{u_i t_s}$ can be calculated in Eq. (3):

$$r'_{u_i t_s} = r_{u_i t_s} + \sum_{u_m \in S_{Ret}(u_i)} p_{t_s}(u_m, u_i) \tag{3}$$

It's easy to find that sum of relevance score of new tags in user u_i is not equal to one and normalization must be taken. The normalized relevance score $r''_{u_i t_s}$ of tag t_s in user u_i is calculated in Eq. (4):

$$r''_{u_i t_s} = r'_{u_i t_s} \Big/ \sum_{t_f \in T'_{u_i}} r'_{u_i t_f} \tag{4}$$

Where T'_{u_i} is the new set of all tags in user u_i.

4   Experiment Evaluation

4.1   Data Sets and Distributed Experimental Environment

The experiments are conducted in a Sina Weibo dataset. The dataset is crawler for about two months which contains 144,210,854 users and 3,052,289,362 relations between users. The interactive graph is built from the 144,210,854 users and 3,052,289,362 relations. We create three test datasets to evaluate the performance of our method. Each test dataset contains 100 users. The relations include both the retweet relationship and notify relationship (Table 1).

We constructed 3 test datasets from the crawled Sina Weibo dataset to test the performance of our method. Since our method is based on the interactive relations between users, we build 3 datasets that has different interactive times with others. Each datasets contains 100 users. Users in the first dataset have 50–60 interactive friends.

Table 1. Sina Weibo Dataset

Property	Number
Users	144,210,854
Relations	3,052,289,362

In the second one, users have 100–150 interactive friends. Users have more than 300 interactive friends in the third one. The performance of our method is evaluated by three volunteers. They are asked to look at top-200 tweets, user profiles and so on to analyze if the tags our method give is right or not. When there is a disagreement between them, the opinion of the majority of them will be considered to be right.

We remove some rare tags in the original dataset. The rare tags are probably caused by mistakes in writing or the tags don't have common meanings. So we remove the tags whose frequency is less than 20 in the original Sina Weibo dataset.

All our experiments are done on an Apache Hadoop[1] cluster which is distributed processing framework of large data sets across clusters of computers. That's because the dataset we use in our experiment is very large that normal server is hard to handle it. Our experimental is conducted in a cluster of computers of hadoop which contains 24 servers. Each server's memory is 32 GB and its CPU is 4-core. The disk of each server is 2 TB. Our data is stored in distributed file system HDFS. All our programs in this paper are based on MapReduce [16] programming model which is for processing large data sets with a parallel, distributed algorithm on a cluster.

4.2   Experiments

To evaluate the performance of our method, three other methods are implemented for mining user personal interests, which are TFIDF method [11], TextRank method [17] and semantic spreading model (SSM) [3]. Traditional keyword extraction approaches TFIDF and TextRank were used to mining personal interests [11]. SSM is proposed to mining user interests based on the Wikipedia semantic graph. The performance of SSM method is according to the paper [3].

For TFIDF method, we first crawl most recent 100 tweets of each user in the dataset using SINA Weibo API and regard the 100 tweets as a whole document. Chinese stemming tools ICTCLAS is used to segment words. We also remove stopwords, emotions and user names. Then the TFIDF value of each keyword is computed and the top-k keywords are considered to be the personal interests tags.

For TextRank method, we also use Chinese stemming tools ICTCLAS to segment words and remove stopwords, emotions and user names. Each nounal keyword is considered to be a vertex and undirected edges are added between two nouns if they co-occur in a tweet. The weight of the edge is set to be the count of the co-occurrence of the the two keywords. The initial values of vertices are arbitrarily set. The value of a vertex is updated according to methods in [17].

---

[1] Apache Hadoop: http://hadoop.apache.org/.

Precision is used to measure the performance the three methods and our method. Top-k tags of each method are evaluated by three volunteers. When there is a disagreement between them, the opinion of the majority of them will be considered to be right. Precision@5 (precision@10) is the average precision of top-5 (top-10) tags in the four methods. Our experiments are conducted in the total of the three dataset. The results are show in Table 2. From the result we can find that our method is much better than traditional keyword extraction approaches TFIDF and TextRank at average precision of top-5 and top-10 tags. Our method is also better than the Wikipedia based SSM method. The results in Table 2 show that our method gets best performance than some classic existing methods.

Table 2. Average precision of the four methods at top-5 and top-10 tags

	TFIDF	TextRank	SSM	Ours
p@5	31.35 %	12.27 %	50.62 %	**71.33 %**
p@10	33.13 %	14.73 %	50 %	**57.6 %**

Since our method is based on the interactive relations between users, we try to analyze the different performance of our method with the change of degree of users. We analyze three groups of users who have 50–60, 100–150 and more than 300 interactive friends which has been discussed in Sect. 4.1. We also evaluate the performance of our method by three volunteers with average precision. Figure 3 shows the results of the three datasets. We can find the users with larger than 300 interactive friends get the worst performance. It's probably because there are too much noisy tags from interactive users. Users with 50–60 interactive friends get better than users with more than 300 friends. Users with 100–150 friends get the best performance, since there are neither too much friends nor too less friends.

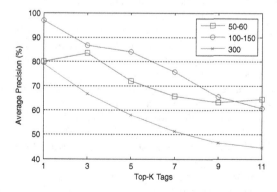

Fig. 3. Different performance of our method with the change of k (the top-k tags) in the three datasets

5   Conclusion and Discussion

In this paper, we propose a user self-defined tags based method to mine user's personal interests. Users with interactive relations are connected to be a weighted directed graph. Our basic hypothesis is that users share potential common interests if they communicate with each other in SINA Weibo. Then user defined tags, which show the personal interests of users, can be propagate from a user to its friends. Our experiments are conducted on a large SINA Weibo datasets in distributed processing framework Hadoop. Experimental results show that our method is better than existing methods. Our method is more efficient since we do not use the content of user's tweets. Furthermore, we analyze the performance of our method with different number of friends. Experimental results show that our method gets best performance when the number of interactive fiends is neither too much nor too less.

Since our method is lightweight because it only employs user self-defined free tags rather than the tweet contents. It can be used in a large social network with even billions of users. The typical applications of our method are friend recommendation, tweet recommendation, detecting domain experts and detecting user communities with the same interests.

In future, we will try to mine user's personal interests based on the content of user's tweets. We also try to combine the methods based on user content and social relations.

Acknowledgment. The research was sponsored by National 973 Program (Grant No. 2013CB329604, 2013CB329601, 2013CB329602), NSFC (Grant No. 60933005, 91124002, 61202362), 863 Program (Grant No. 2012AA01A401, 2012AA01A402), National Key Technology R&D Program (Grant No. 2012BAH38B04, 2012BAH38B06).

References

1. Bhattacharya, P., et al.: Inferring user interests in the Twitter social network. In: Proceedings of the 8th ACM Conference on Recommender Systems. ACM (2014)
2. Claypool, M., et al.: Inferring user interests. Internet Comput. IEEE **5**(6), 32–39 (2001)
3. Fan, M., Zhou, Q., Zheng, T.F.: Mining the personal interests of microbloggers via exploiting wikipedia knowledge. In: Gelbukh, A. (ed.) CICLing 2014, Part II. LNCS, vol. 8404, pp. 188–200. Springer, Heidelberg (2014)
4. Li, H.: Mining User Interest in Microblogs with a User-Topic Model (2013)
5. Li, X., Guo, L., Zhao, Y.E.: Tag-based social interests discovery. In: Proceedings of the 17th International Conference on World Wide Web. ACM (2008)
6. Michelson, M., Macskassy, S.A.: Discovering users' topics of interests on twitter: a first look. In: Proceedings of the Fourth Workshop on Analytics for Noisy Unstructured Text Data 2010, pp. 73–80. ACM, Toronto (2010)
7. Xu, Z., et al.: Discovering user interest on twitter with a modified author-topic model. In: IEEE/WIC/ACM International Conference on Web Intelligence and Intelligent Agent Technology (WI-IAT), 2011. IEEE (2011)
8. Liu, Z., Chen, X., Sun, M.: Mining the interests of Chinese microbloggers via keyword extraction. Front. Comput. Sci. **6**(1), 76–87 (2012)

9. Shen, W., et al.: Linking named entities in Tweets with knowledge base via user interests modeling. In: Proceedings of the 19th ACM SIGKDD International Conference on Knowledge Discovery and Data Mining 2013, pp. 68–76. ACM, Chicago (2013)
10. Rosen-Zvi, M., et al.: Learning author-topic models from text corpora. ACM Trans. Inf. Syst. (TOIS) **28**(1), 4 (2010)
11. Wu, W., Zhang, B., Ostendorf, M.: Automatic generation of personalized annotation tags for twitter users. in Human Language Technologies. In: The 2010 Annual Conference of the North American Chapter of the Association for Computational Linguistics. Association for Computational Linguistics (2010)
12. Xiang, W., et al.: Improving text categorization with semantic knowledge in Wikipedia. IEICE Trans. Inf. Syst. **96**(12), 2786–2794 (2013)
13. Wang, X., et al.: Computing semantic relatedness using chinese wikipedia links and taxonomy. J. Chin. Comput. Syst. **32**(11), 2237–2242 (2011)
14. Michelson, M., Macskassy, S.A.: Discovering users' topics of interest on twitter: a first look. In: Proceedings of the Fourth Workshop on Analytics for Noisy Unstructured Text Data. ACM (2010)
15. Gabrilovich, E., Markovitch, S.: Computing semantic relatedness using Wikipedia-based explicit semantic analysis. In: Proceedings of the 20th International Joint Conference on Artifical Intelligence 2007, pp. 1606–1611. Morgan Kaufmann Publishers Inc., Hyderabad (2007)
16. Dean, J., Ghemawat, S.: MapReduce: simplified data processing on large clusters. Commun. ACM **51**(1), 107–113 (2008)
17. Mihalcea, R., Tarau, P.: TextRank: bringing order into texts. In: Proceedings of EMNLP, Barcelona, Spain (2004)

Social Media Usage as a Service: A Service-Dominant Logic Perspective

Tao Hu[1,2](✉) and Hengjie Wang[2](✉)

[1] School of Applied Science and Technology, King University,
1350 King College Road, Bristol, TN 37620, USA
thu@king.edu
[2] School of Business Administration, Qingdao Binhai University,
425 West Jialingjiang Road, Qingdao, Shandong 266555, China
frankwhj@126.com

Abstract. The wide use and distinctive novelties of social media have established the ever pervasive phenomenon a "hot topic" for information systems (IS) research and practice. In this regard, the Service-Dominant (S-D) Logic from the services marketing literature supports the notion that social media users and providers interact with each other and co-create the platform for benefit needs. In this paper, we applied the S-D Logic perspective to the specific usage context of social media. We developed a conceptual framework theorizing social media usage as a service in terms of service provision mechanisms, value propositions and co-creation, and associated value co-creation behaviors. The conceptual framework bears important implications for IS theory in enriching social media research in specific and elaborating the cumulative tradition of IS research in general. It also has practical and design implications for social media firms in improving long term survivability.

Keywords: Social media · Service-Dominant Logic · Value · Co-creation

1 Introduction

Recent years have witnessed the high popularity and wide use of social media for personal and organizational purposes around the world. Even so, the rise and fall of social media has been widely reported. For social media firms, the long-term corporate profitability and viability is heavily dependent on a critical mass of active participative users [1, 2]. Therefore, it is critical for social media practitioners to gain a deeper understanding of how social media are configured, used as a service, and create value.

In the Information Systems (IS) research area, the widespread use of social media has established a "hot topic" calling for the systematic investigations into the ever pervasive phenomenon [3, 4]. Identifying implications of social media use for both IS research and practice, however, is still challenging [5, 6]. The challenge is largely attributed to the interactions of key social media players and information technology (IT) artifacts [4], and reflect the dual role people play in the use of social media as service customers and users of IT artifacts as well [7, 8].

© Springer International Publishing Switzerland 2015
X. Xiao and Z. Zhang (Eds.): WAIM 2015, LNCS 9391, pp. 88–99, 2015.
DOI: 10.1007/978-3-319-23531-8_8

The aforementioned phenomena have led to two research questions this paper attempts to address, (1) how can we theorize the nature and value creation of social media usage? And (2) what implications and consequences does social media usage bear for IS practitioners and organizations? This necessitates the development of new theoretical perspectives in line with the specific usage setting of social media [4, 5].

As to our best knowledge, IS research has not paid sufficient attention specifically on the theorization of social media usage, and yet realized the theoretical and practical importance of establishing theory-driven perspectives for deeper understanding of the phenomenon [4, 5]. In this regard, the Service-Dominant (S-D) Logic from the services marketing literature provides valuable points of view that support the notion that key social media players interact with each other and co-create the platform for benefit needs. Starting from this perspective, this paper represents our first attempt applying the S-D Logic to the specific usage context of social media. We develop a conceptual framework theorizing social media usage as a service in terms of service provision mechanisms, value propositions and co-creation, and associated value co-creation behaviors. We believe the proposed framework has important implications for IS research and practice.

The paper is organized as follows. The next section summarizes the S-D Logic perspective and paves the theoretical foundation for developing a conceptual framework of social media usage as a service. The characteristics of social media are then reviewed, and the S-D Logic is applied to the specific context of social media. Subsequently, research propositions and a conceptual framework are developed from the S-D Logic perspective outlining the characteristics and major relationships of social media usage as a service. The last section discusses theoretical, practical and design implications of viewing social media usage as a service, as well as future research questions and agendas in this direction.

2 Theory: Service-Dominant Logic

The seminal work of the S-D Logic was published in [9]. Since then, it is generally believed that the S-D Logic provides a valuable theoretical perspective that necessitates the re-evaluation of the conventional literature of innovations [10]. We next summarize the S-D Logic from the seminal work of [9,11–14], and show that the perspective can be applied to the specific context of social media to enrich our understanding of usage nature and consequences of the technology.

2.1 Service Definition

The S-D Logic defines service as "the application of specialized competences (skills and knowledge), through deeds, processes, and performances for the benefit of another entity or the entity itself (self-service)." [11] Here service is viewed as a series of managerial and marketing activities and processes in which customers and provider firms collaborate to produce a service through exchange of specialized skills, knowledge, competences and resources, and co-create value for service use. In the process, provider firms apply and integrate their competences and resources with those of potential customers to make value propositions; and as customers encounter and make use of the service, they proactively perceive, co-create and realize the value for their unique needs. The process renders an interactive relationship between customers and providers that generates value for both parties.

2.2 Service Resources and Types

The S-D Logic classifies resources into operand and operant ones. The former refers to the physical tangible "stuff" such as goods, money, and natural resources; the latter refers to the intangible dynamic functions of human ingenuity, knowledge, competence, and organizational processes that can generate effects and additional resources. The S-D Logic believes a service is produced and delivered by applying and integrating various resources, in which "operations or acts are performed to (operand) resources that produce effects." [9] Here the S-D Logic underlies the primary importance of operant resources that the provider firms focus on to make value propositions for a service.

The above resource classification suggests two types of service depending on the way how physical tangible goods are involved in the provision and use of a service. Firstly, a service (e.g., education, banking, consulting, etc.) may be co-produced, and value co-created and used directly through the exchange of core competences and resources to the extent that tangible physical goods are less involved. And secondly, when tangible physical goods (e.g., retailing, dining, IS, etc.) are more involved, they are viewed as appliances/means serving as an enabling distribution platform/mechanism that customers learn to adapt and interact with to render the provision and use of the service. For both types of service, "the application of specialized skills and knowledge is the fundamental unit of exchange between service providers and customers." [9]

2.3 Service Value

The S-D Logic defines service value as "an improvement in system well-being" that can be measured in terms of "a system's adaptiveness or ability to fit in its environment." [14] In this light, service value represents wealth to better the circumstances, and solutions to customers' problems and for support. In the specific contexts, service value is realized as various effectively utilizable benefits and advantages (value-in-context) at higher order. This implies that customers are endogenous to the creation of service value.

For customers, service benefits are perceived "wants" and "satisfaction" for higher order needs such as usefulness, self-fulfillment and esteem, and "valued states of being such as happiness, convenience, security, and accomplishment." [15] And for provider firms, service value is learned and improved from the interactive relationship with customers. It is reflected in business behaviors and performances that provider firms can seek to maximize the lifetime benefits.

2.4   Co-creation of Service Value

The S-D Logic contends that service provision and use reflects the process of value co-creation through resource collaborations of customers and providers. The S-D Logic largely stresses the critical role that customers play as an operant resource in creating a service, value of which is generated by its use, and thus "is defined by and co-created with the customer" [9]. According to the S-D Logic, the roles of the provider and customer in service provision and use are not distinct. Rather, service value is co-created jointly and reciprocally through the interactions of both parties and integration of competences and resources of the two parties.

Specifically, service value is co-created through the collaborated efforts of both providers and customers, and is determined by the two parties. At the inception of a service, providers apply their competences and resources to make value propositions for service offerings. Customers are connected to the providers through the encounter of value propositions. They may accept the value propositions for their own lives, and are actively engaged in producing and delivering the service through integrating their competence and resources. Moreover, Customers continue the value-creation through their use and maintenance of the service. In the process, customers and providers co-create value reciprocally contributing resources, knowledge, skills, and relationships to the performance of service marketing, delivery and use.

3   Social Media Usage as a Service

3.1   An Overview of Social Media

In this paper, we define social media technically as an integrative collection of mobile and wireless/wired telecommunication and computing technologies. Functionally, social media build on the creation and exchange of user generated content to meet people's social needs for informational and relational connections. Behind the advances of social media has been the universal standards-based integration of what are commonly termed Web 2.0 technologies. The integrated infrastructure of Web 2.0 technologies genetically encompass a wide range of collaboration and ease of information sharing across multiple modes of human communications, and hence is viewed as a participatory and interactive platform. As such, social media transcend far from an information resource to a user-centric platform on which various user-generated contents are deployed and processed.

Social media applications have four built-in features to meet users' social needs [3, 4]. (1) Constructing a public or semi-public user profile. Indeed, the profile of social media provides users with an opportunity to "type oneself into being." [16] (2) Articulating a list of users for informational and relational connections. This function of social media allows users to build an aggregated list of virtual networks for social interactions. (3) Viewing and traversing virtual connections. This allows users to manage and keep control over information search and relation development. And, (4) getting access to user generated contents. The desire to access, communicate and share online contents has been viewed as the primary driver of social media usage [3].

Researchers have differentiated the technical and functional characteristics of social media from those of traditional media surrounding ubiquity, flexibility, voluntary easy use, and individual empowerment [3, 4, 17, 18]. These differences fully reflect the theoretical novelties of social media. In this paper, we propose that social media usage be considered as a service that is proposed, delivered, and used in the ongoing relationships between users and providers. That is, social media usage embodies and hence is a specific case of service value proposition, co-creation, and exchange in an organizational setting. We next apply the S-D Logic to the specific context of social media to develop a conceptual framework outlining the characteristics and relationships of social media usage as a service.

3.2 Developing a Conceptual Framework of Social Media Usage

3.2.1 Social Media as a Service Platform

Through the lens of the S-D Logic, the features of social media are built and delivered upon the application of a wide variety of specialized skills, knowledge, and competences of technical and managerial players in an organizational setting. At the technical aspect, social media designers, analysts and programmers contribute their professional competences and performance in programming, networking, and computer hardware and software to build seamless connectivity and transformability across interconnected networking nodes. The organizational deeds configure the technical features of the platform and make it usable so that users can read, write, and meet in a participative way, and are further enabled to interact and collaborate as creators of user-generated contents. It is the technology of know-how (technical skills, knowledge, core competences, and resources) that builds social media as an artificial platform – a technical appliance, on and through which users achieve usage experience and enjoy informational and relational connections it renders.

Moreover, as the social media platform is built with technical features, the firm mangers and marketing employees step in. They formulate managerial and marketing strategies, and implement management technology (i.e., management procedures associated with business administration), based on which value propositions are made in defining and meeting users' social needs. From the perspective of business operations, the technical and managerial actors including designers, managers, executives, and all levels of employees serve as the corporate operant resources, and act on the social media platform for the production, delivery, and performance of social media service. They coordinate skills, knowledge, and competences with each other to implement the technical functions of social media, and form a service system to market and maintain the platform in the right condition to deliver expected value.

It is in the above sense that social media function as an intermediate conduit embedding core competences of key players. And furthermore, the set of organizational processes and activities orchestrates to make social media usable in the market and ensure users understand and accept the value propositions, and eventually make use of the application.

Proposition 1 (P1):

> *Social media function as a service platform that embeds skills, knowledge, competences, and resources of technical and managerial players and users who serve as the operant resources for the production, delivery, and performance of social media.*

3.2.2   Value of Social Media

The S-D Logic contends that service usage creates value to improve the adaptability and survivability for both customers and providers. The value of social media use is specifically manifested as translatable benefits and advantages for both parties. [7] summarizes customer value of social media as defining and meeting users' higher order needs for informational and relational connections such as (1) the life sense of social identities and belongingness; (2) information searching and sharing for support and as survival solutions; (3) intrinsic enjoyment and relaxation; and (4) self-presentation of status and image.

Proposition 2 (P2):

> *Value of social media use for users is manifested as translatable benefits and advantages in defining and meeting users' higher-order needs for informational and relational connections.*

Meanwhile, social media providers learn and obtain value from the interactive relationship with users and their active use of the technology. For the provider firms, social media value is realized as the improvement in overall corporate performance in such aspects as cost-efficiency, customer responsiveness, advertising gains, marketing extension, and long-term survival [17]. The long-term viability and marketing success of social media firms is heavily dependent on a critical mass of continued user of the service [17, 19]. Besides, social media providers can harness the activities of users generating content to create business value [20].

Proposition 3 (P3):

> *Value of social media use for provider firms is realized as the improvement in overall business performance in such aspects as cost-efficiency, customer responsiveness, advertising gains, marketing extension, and long-term survival.*

3.2.3   Value Co-creation of Social Media

Through the lens of the S-D Logic, social media providers define and co-create value with users rather than simply embed it in its technical features or management technologies. In the process, as users play a critical role in configuring technical features of the service platform, users' value co-creation takes place early in the value proposition process even before value is realized. In the course of social media construction, users contribute their benefit perceptions and specialized competences that social media providers integrate with the competences and resources of their own to propose desirable value of the application.

Further through marketing surveys and relational interactions, social media designers learn the problems, solution, and benefit needs that users want to address through the application. Based on the findings, provider firms leverage their competences and resources, and build the platform embedding value propositions to fit users' needs. Therefore, in the value proposition process, users co-create value through sharing their inventiveness, insights, and knowledge with designers. The co-created value at the value proposition stage is reflected in the configuration of key technical features, and managerial and marketing processes of social media.

Proposition 4 (P4):

Social media provider firms leverage their competences and resources, and build the service platform that embeds value propositions to fit users' social needs.

Proposition 5 (P5):

In the value proposition process, social media users co-create value through sharing inventiveness, insights, and knowledge with designers. The co-created value at this stage is reflected in the configuration of key technical features, and managerial and marketing processes of social media.

Furthermore, as users accept the value propositions and start using the application, they continue to co-create value through their usage behavior. Increasingly, users are actively engaged in value co-creation by cooperating with the provider and by serving themselves as well. For the former, as the provider serves users and improves performance, users cooperate with the provider to create corporate value through their usage activities and the interactive relationship. For the latter, users' informational and relational activities and creation of user contents generate value for themselves. The structural integration of Web 2.0 technologies constructs the service platform and enables users to create value for all participants as they use it.

Proposition 6 (P6):

Users continue to co-create value of social media through their use of the application by cooperating with social media providers and by serving themselves as well.

Therefore, the value co-creation of social media embeds users' perceptions and behaviors in both value propositions and actual use of the application. On the one hand, users devote knowledge, competences, and time and effort for value propositions; they maintain and adapt the social media for their usage situation and unique needs. Users' collaborative role in co-producing and making use of social media makes them primarily an operant resource and a value creator for the provider firm. On the other hand, users' perceptions and usage activities co-create social value for themselves. There can be no value without users incorporating the firm offering into their own life and contexts. Users' co-creation of value makes them endogenous to the whole value chain system of social media throughout the development, marketing, delivery, and use of the service.

Proposition 7 (P7):

> *In the value co-creation, specialized skills, knowledge, competences, and resources of key social media players including providers, employees, and users are the fundamental basis of exchange paving the base for their interactive relationship.*

3.2.4   Value Co-creation Behaviors of Social Media

Building upon an extensive literature review, [21] proposes a typology of value co-creation behaviors of social media users as follows. *(1) Relationship developing.* Social media users are engaged in various social networking activities to maintain and develop relationships with friends, colleagues, and even virtual avatars. *(2) Information sharing.* Among a large pool of contacts and contents, social media construct a rich source of information channels for users to search and share information and social events. *(3) Self-presenting.* Social media users craft profiles and situations to present social status and image of themselves in a preferred manner [22]. And, *(4) entertaining.* Social media were originally developed to satisfy people's personal needs for enjoyment and relaxation. The informational, relational, and self-presenting interactions in social media are embellished so well as to carry hedonic entertaining experience.

It is worthwhile to note that the proposed value co-creation behaviors are conceptually symbiotic and interrelated, and, as a group, jointly define the underlying nature of value co-creation activities of social media [17]. Each of the four behaviors is conceptually distinct from others, and defines a unique prominent aspect of value co-creation activities of social media.

Proposition 8 (P8):

> *Value co creation behaviors of social media users can be categorized as relationship developing, information sharing, self-presenting, and entertaining. These behaviors are conceptually symbiotic and interrelated, and, as a group, jointly define the underlying nature of value co-creation activities of social media.*

3.2.5   A Conceptual Framework of Social Media Usage as a Service

Summarizing the above propositions, we developed a conceptual framework from the S-D Logic perspective outlining the characteristics and relationships of social media usage as a service. As shown in Fig. 1, the framework identifies three components of social media usage – providers, users, and social media itself, and describes the interactions of the three components. The framework shows that social media as a service platform is co-produced with the collaborations of both provider firms and users through the application and exchange of specialized skills, knowledge, competences, and resources of both parties (P1). The framework suggests that social media provider firms make value propositions through integrating users' participation and contributions (P4). The framework further indicates that users determine and co-create social media value (P5, P6) for both parties (P2, P3) through a variety of usage behaviors (P8). Finally, the framework maintains that social media providers and users are interrelated in the process of value propositions and co-creation; they further develop an interactive relationship on the basis of exchange of specialized skills, knowledge, competences, and resources (P7).

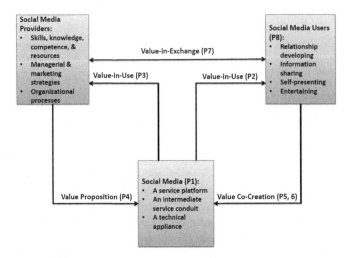

Fig. 1. The conceptual framework of social media usage as a service

4 Discussion

4.1 Implications for IS Research

The novel and distinctive issues highlighted by the conceptual framework have important theoretical implications for IS research. Addressing the dual role people play in the use of social media as service customers and users of IT artifacts, the framework is intended to identify key constructs and interactions of social media providers, users, and IT artifacts. This raises important research questions and agenda surrounding the production, delivery, and use of social media service.

The primary contribution of this paper to IS research is to articulate a vision from the S-D logic perspective for and a roadmap of the researchable questions and agendas for IS scholars to investigate fundamental theoretical issues that are raised when social media is used as a service. The constructs and relationships encompassed in the conceptual framework involve the core issues of IS research including how the social media platform is technically co-produced and implemented, how social media are used to co-create value to meet benefit needs of providers and users, and how the service use impacts perceptions and behaviors of both parties. Investigations of these issues in the ever ubiquitous novel context should facilitate deeper insights about these phenomena. Research in this direction will largely enrich our understanding of social media usage as a service in specific, and help re-evaluate key IS phenomena in general and elaborate the cumulative tradition of IS research.

Moreover, future research may consider to theoretically elaborate the research constructs and operationalize them into measurable variables, specify the set of research propositions into concrete hypotheses, and collect data in specific empirical contexts. As these goals are achieved appropriately, the conceptual framework can be validated empirically, and further generalized as an overarching model to investigate social media usage in various alternative settings. The conceptualizations of key constructs and relationships in specific contexts can illustrate that the conceptual framework may serve as a foundational model informing research in the broader contexts of social media usage.

4.2   Implications for IS Practice

The conceptual framework bears important managerial implications for IS practice, especially for social media firms and organizational users to improve service quality and effectiveness for the long-term business adaptability and survivability. The conceptualization of social media usage as a service highlights the critical role of users, and counts users as a primary corporate operant resource in the delivery and use of the service. The conceptualization establishes a solid base for social media designers and managers to perceive and approach to users and achieve an overarching customer centric marketing strategy in the pursuit of the following managerial goals.

(1) *Establish long-term interactive relationship with users.* The conceptual framework suggests that managers and designers iteratively interact with users and establish a long-term view of user relationships. For this purpose, strategies such as marketing transparency and information symmetry in the delivery and use of social media help designers and managers maintain communications and intimacy with users and sustain the longitudinal relationships [9].

(2) *Make right and better value propositions.* To sustain a critical mass of active participative users, social media firms should focus on the configuration and delivery of social media applications, and propose right and better service value to fit users' benefit needs. To meet this end, managers and designers can build prototyping applications and invite users to try out, and observe how users react to the hypothesized meanings embedded in the design [10].

(3) *Identify meaningful value co-creation behaviors.* The conceptual framework suggests that, across various social media applications, users may display a variety of behaviors in co-creating usage value; and user value co-creation is critical for marketing success of social media firms. Keeping this in mind, managers and designers should identify users' value co-creation behaviors for different social media applications, and figure out what usage behavior matters most for users' value perceptions and needs. Based on this insight, managers and designers can design and customize service features to enhance users' value co-creation activities and performance of social media.

(4) Finally, as organizations and companies use social media to better understand customer orientation and consumer value [18], the organizations mostly play the user role to co-create value in an organizational setting. In this light, the conceptual framework lays a groundwork that helps organizational users understand how to make sense of the social media ecology, and develop strategies for monitoring and responding to social media activities to co-create value for the organizational performance.

4.3 Design Implications in and for Social Ubiquitous Networking Environments

Finally, the conceptual framework bears important design implications in and for social ubiquitous networking environments where social media are widely used as a service platform and social recommendation systems are built as one of the most important components for service providers and users to interact with each other. In this aspect, our design recommendations include, (1) fully consider the dual roles of provider firms and users as an operant resource and an operand resource in proposing, creating and delivering social media as a service; (2) create and configure social media as a service platform that firm actors and users can take full advantage of the conduit and technical flexibility and autonomy to exchange skills, knowledge and competencies; (3) build a transparent service innovation ecosystem that provider firms and users are strongly encouraged to collaborate and exchange and co-create value for each other; and (4) a recommendation system that is built in and for a social ubiquitous networking environment should fully capture the interactions of key players and social media artifacts, and reflect the set of usage behaviors in relationship developing, information sharing, self-presenting, and entertaining.

5   Conclusion

Information systems are embodied in the ways people create value with information and relationship, so are social media. In this paper, we developed a conceptual framework outlining in depth the characteristics and relationships of social media usage as a service and addressing the interactions of key players social media usage. As the most significant impact and implications of social media for individuals and organizations are still to come, we believe the conceptual framework makes important contributions to IS research and social media practice in helping us understand and re-evaluate the the sociotechnical context of IS value creation.

References

1. Powell, J.: 33 Million People in the Room: How to Create, Influence, and Run a Successful Business with Social Networking. FT Press, New Jerzy (2009)
2. Sledgianowski, D., Kulviwat, S.: Using social network sites: the effects of playfulness, critical mass and trust in a hedonic context. J. Comput. Inf. Syst. **49**, 74–83 (2009)
3. Ellison, N.B., Boyd, D.M.: Sociality through social network sites. In: Dutton, W.H. (ed.) The Oxford Handbook of Internet Studies, pp. 151–172. Oxford University Press, Oxford (2013)
4. Kane, G., Alavi, M., Labianca, G., Borgatti, S.P.: What's different about social media networks? a framework and research agenda. MIS Q. **38**, 275–304 (2014)
5. Aral, S., Dellarocas, C., Godes, D.: Social media and business transformation: a framework for research. Inf. Syst. Res. **24**, 3–13 (2013)

6. Sundararajan, A., Provost, F., Oestreicher-Singer, G., Aral, S.: Information in digital, economic, and social media. Inf. Syst. Res. **24**, 883–905 (2013)

7. Hu, T., Kettinger, W., Poston, R.: The effect of online social value on satisfaction and continued use of social media. Eur. J. Inf. Syst. **24**(4), 391–410 (2014)

8. Kim, H., Chan, H.C., Gupta, S.: Value-based adoption of mobile internet: an empirical investigation. Decis. Support Syst. **43**, 111–126 (2007)

9. Vargo, S.L., Lusch, R.F.: Evolving to a new dominant logic for marketing. J. Mark. **68**, 1–17 (2004)

10. Michel, S., Brown, S.W., Gallan, A.S.: An expanded and strategic view of discontinuous innovations: developing a Service-Dominant logic. J. Acad. Mark. Sci. **36**, 54–66 (2008)

11. Vargo, S.L., Lusch, R.F.: The four service marketing myths: remnants of a goods-based, manufacturing model. J. Serv. Res. **6**, 324–335 (2004)

12. Vargo, S.L., Lusch, R.F.: Why service? J. Acad. Mark. Sci. **36**, 35–38 (2008)

13. Vargo, S.L., Lusch, R.F.: Service-Dominant logic: continuing the evolution. J. Acad. Mark. Sci. **36**, 1–10 (2008)

14. Vargo, S.L., Maglio, P., Akaka, M.: On value and value co-creation: a service systems and service logic perspective. Eur. Manag. J. **26**, 145–152 (2008)

15. Gutman, J.: A Means–end chain model based on consumer categorization processes. J. Mark. **46**, 60–72 (1982)

16. Boyd, D.M., Ellison, N.B.: Social network sites: definition, history, and scholarship. J. Comput. Mediated Commun. **13**, 210–230 (2007)

17. Ahlqvist, T., Bäck, A., Halonen, M., Heinonen, S.: Social Media Road Maps Exploring the Futures Triggered by Social Media. VTT Tiedotteita – Valtion Teknillinen Tutkimuskeskus, 13 (2008)

18. Kaplan, A.M., Haenlein, M.: Users of the world, unite! the challenges and opportunities of social media. Bus. Horiz. **53**, 59–68 (2010)

19. Bhattacherjee, A., Perols, J., Sanford, C.: Information technology continuance: a theoretical extension and empirical test. J. Comput. Inf. Syst. **49**, 17–26 (2008)

20. O'Reilly, T. Battelle, J.: Opening Welcome: State of the Internet Industry. Web 2.0 Conference San Francisco, California, 5 October 2004

21. Hu, T., Zhang, P., Gao, G., Jiao, S., Ke, J., Lian, Y.: Specify usage of social media as a formative construct: theory and implications for higher education. In: Li, S., Jin, Q., Jiang, X., Park, J.J.(J.H.) (eds.) Frontier and Future Development of Information Technology. Lecture Notes in Electrical Engineering, vol. 269, pp. 565–578. Springer, Netherlands (2013)

22. Kim, H., Chan, H.C., Kankanhalli, A.: What motivates people to purchase digital items on virtual community websites? the desire for online self-presentation. Inf. Syst. Res. **23**, 1232–1245 (2012)

Information Revelation for Better or Worse Recommendation: Understanding Chinese Users' Privacy Attitudes and Practices

Tiffany Y. Tang[(⊠)]

Media Lab, Department of Computer Science, Wenzhou-Kean University,
Wenzhou, China
yatang@kean.edu

Abstract. The performance of a Recommendation System (RS) is mainly determined by how well it 'understands' its users: how much information it is able to trace and obtain. The former is largely depended on the *algorithmic* designs of the recommendation which have been explored for over a decade, while the former is more and more determined by the data owners—the users. In this paper, we presented our study on understanding Chinese users' information revelation attitudes and practices which has not been fully explored in both the recommendation and online privacy research fields. Specifically, unlike the majority of previous studies that revealed users' self-disclosure practices and attitudes in SNSs, our study is the first and only an initial investigation into the two aspects of the personal information disclosure and sharing: the differences of personal information shared by and with different types of audiences. Our study revealed that among the five types of recipient's, students placed the least trust on Advertisers, among four other groups as Close Friends and Family, University Community, Friends on the Social Networking Sites, and Complete (online) Strangers. Overall, students feel more comfortable actively sharing personal information with the types of audiences than being shared by these audiences of their personal details.

Keywords: Disclosure · Recommendation system · Privacy attitude · Privacy practice

1 Introduction

The performance of a Recommendation System (RS) is mainly determined by how well it 'understands' its users: how much information it is able to trace and obtain. The former is largely depended on the algorithmic designs of the recommendation which have been explored for over a decade, while the former is more and more determined by the data owners—the users. In this paper, we presented our study on understanding Chinese users' information revelation attitudes and practices which has not been fully explored in both the recommendation and online privacy research fields. Specifically, unlike the majority of previous studies that revealed users' self-disclosure practices and attitudes in SNSs (Livingstone 2006; Stein and Sinha 2002; Utz and Kramer 2009; Taddicken 2013; Barnes 2006; Gross and Acquisti 2005; Thelwall 2008; Lewis et al. 2008; Govani and Pashley

© Springer International Publishing Switzerland 2015
X. Xiao and Z. Zhang (Eds.): WAIM 2015, LNCS 9391, pp. 100–112, 2015.
DOI: 10.1007/978-3-319-23531-8_9

2005; Solove 2013, among many others), our study is the first and only an initial investigation into the two aspects of the personal information disclosure and sharing: the differences of personal information shared *by* and *with* different types of audiences.

Livingstone (2006) refer to *privacy* as the ability that one has control over who knows what about them; Stein and Sinha's (2002) defined privacy as '*the rights of individuals to enjoy autonomy, to be left alone, and to determine whether and how information about one's self is revealed to others*' (p. 414). The differences regarding what constitutes privacy lead to a wide variety of active researches on privacy attitudes, patterns and how they would have effect privacy practices and behaviors (among many others, (Livingstone 2006; Stein and Sinha 2002; Utz and Kramer 2009; Taddicken 2013; Barnes 2006; Gross and Acquisti 2005; Thelwall 2008; Lewis et al. 2008; Govani and Pashley 2005; Solove 2013)). In summary, privacy is multi-faceted and has been famously and notoriously regarded as a *commodity* instead of a *right* (Acquisti 2004; Acquisti and Grossklags 2005; Acquisti et al. 2009). Consequently, it is well-known that users have difficulties reconciling their desire to be open and reluctance to reveal certain 'private' information (Taddicken 2013; Gross and Acquisti 2005; Thelwall 2008; Lewis et al. 2008; Govani and Pashley 2005), a famous phenomenon known as *privacy paradox* (Gross and Acquisti 2005).

Fundamental to privacy paradox is the *recontextualization* of *self-disclosure* (Taddicken 2013): social network audiences are heterogeneous and constitutes different social relationships with the data owner, for example, childhood close friends, friends on the SNS, family, classmates etc., a phenomenon is known as '*context collapse*' (Marwick and Boyd 2011). Previous research reported the differences in the granularity of disclosures people are comfortable with (Lin et al. 2013); in particular how users are comfortable with sharing work and home location information to different types of recipients.

Unlike previous studies that revealed users' self-disclosure practices in SNSs, we go steps further by differentiating the types of audiences with whom users revealed their personal information, which is one of the main contribution of this study. To the best of our knowledge, our study is one of the few unfolding the level and granularities of information revealing attitudes and practices among Chinese college students who are studying in an American university. In addition, there are very few works studying users' awareness of subject knowledge on the programmability of certain privacy information, which motivates our study here.

It is our hope that our study can add richness to the understanding of the level and granularities of information revealing attitudes and preferences, as well as lending credence to the explanations of privacy paradox.

The remaining of this paper is organized as follows. Background and related works will be presented in Sect. 2, followed by the detailed discussions on our study in Sect. 3. Findings will be reported in the same section. In Sect. 4, we offer to provide discussions on the experiment results as well as the design implications to the RS community. Finally, we conclude this paper by pointing out the limitations of our study and our future work.

2 Related Works

Although various social network sites share the core purpose of facilitating online interaction/communication and information sharing, with varied goals, users might behave differently. In this section, we will survey previous research efforts related to our current study.

2.1 Privacy Concerns and Disclosure in SNSs in General

There is a rich body of research studies as well as media attention on internet users' privacy concerns (among many others, Livingstone 2006; Stein and Sinha 2002; Utz and Kramer 2009; Taddicken 2013; Barnes 2006; Gross and Acquisti 2005; Thelwall 2008; Lewis et al. 2008; Govani and Pashley 2005; Solove 2013). These studies investigate various aspects of privacy issues on the social network sites, from privacy revealing patterns (Gross and Acquisti 2005, Lin et al. 2013), information self-disclosure practices (Fogel and Nehmad 2009; Tufekci 2008; Stutzman et al. 2011; Zhao and Jiang 2011, Acquisti and Gross 2006), to the link between privacy revealing and users' internet behaviors from behavioral economics' perspective (Acquisti and Grossklags 2005, 2007).

Fairly speaking, the majority of current studies focus on western users' behaviors, attitudes, and preferences on internet privacy, therefore, the extent to which these findings generalize to other regions, such as East Asian, is still an open question (Lin et al. 2013; Wang et al. 2011). Recently, with the exponential growth of netizens in China, interests on whether or not Western users and their Chinese counterpart differ have sparked a number of studies (among them, Lin et al. 2013; Ur and Wang 2013; Yoo and Huang 2011, Zhao and Jiang 2011; Wang et al. 2011). For example, there is a number of studies reported that American users are more stable in disclosing location-based information during weekends, while Chinese users exhibits fluctuating patterns in sharing these information (Lin et al. 2013, Wang et al. 2011; Ur and Wang 2013). While Chinese users are more conservative in self-disclosure in SNSs, American users were more concerned with privacy than Chinese and Indian users (Wang et al. 2011). Zhao and Jiang (2011) reported different behaviors between American and Chinese students' handling of public profile images in Facebook: almost all 57 Chinese participants customize their profile in order to 'impersonalized' themselves, while 35 % of their US counterparts (57 in total) used group photos for their profile image.

Lin et al. (2013) compared the location-sharing privacy preferences between Chinese and American university students. While their findings revealed that both groups share many similarities in information revealing preferences, they differ in the level of personal information to be shared with different groups of people/organizations. For instance, US students were significantly more comfortable about sharing their location at 'work' than their location at 'home'; but Chinese students are being equally concerned in revealing both locations (Lin et al. 2013).

Stutzman et al. (2011) pointed out that privacy behaviors and privacy policy consumption have an impact on users' privacy attitudes and therefore explain their self-disclosure practices on Facebook. They suggest transparent privacy policies and privacy controls to mitigate users' privacy concerns. A recent study further shows that while users are aware of the contents of the shared information; they often exhibit ignorance on the visibility of the information (Moll et al. 2014), which is consistent with the effect of asymmetric information as observed in the behavioral economics field (Akerlof 1970). This underestimation could also help explain the privacy paradox.

2.2 Privacy Paradox

Privacy paradox does exist. The paradox refers to the concept that while users care about their online privacy, they tend not to do anything to control it (Utz and Kramer 2009; Taddicken 2013; Utz and Kramer 2009; Barnes 2006; Gross and Acquisti 2005; Thelwall 2008; Lewis et al. 2008; Govani and Pashley 2005). While Utz and Kramer (2009) did not provide any explanations over why this happens; Solove (2013) argued that privacy control should be more appropriately discussed not at the individual level but at a collective level due to the complexity of structural elements that contribute to the privacy control. In other words, the cognitive loads on which the privacy control settings have been put on an individual is enormous.

Moreover, privacy is more addressed in a series of isolated translations by an individual entity's privacy self-management; therefore, it is hard as well as inappropriate to assess the privacy costs and benefits. Hence, some researchers started to look into this problem from the behavioral economics' perspective. In particular, prior studies agreed on the discrepancy between privacy attitudes and privacy behaviors (Acquisti 2004, Wathieu and Friedman 2005; Norberg et al. 2007), especially regarding the dramatic gap between users' "willingness to pay" to protect the privacy of their data and their "willingness to accept" money in order to give up privacy protection (Acquisti et al. 2009, pp. 3).

2.3 The Granularity of Privacy Information Disclosure

Users' lack of metacognitive knowledge of the potential audiences of their personal information might explain the privacy paradox. However, our understanding of this issue is at an early stage. Among the bulk of previous studies very few focused on it.

As one of the first few studies examining the accessibility spectrum of users' information disclosure behaviors, Utz and Kramer (2009) ran a survey to look into the privacy accessibility by friends, friends of friends, and Hyvers/everybody, and found out that compared between sharing with friends and friends of friends, most of them are comfortable sharing their last name (32 % vs. 8 %), email address (51 % vs. 6 %), cell-phone number (34 % vs. 3 %), photos (40.5 % vs. 17 %) . They did not however, study such target users as advertisers, people on campus etc.

Lin et al. (2013) tackled the same problem, though focusing on users' location-sharing preferences among American and Chinese university students. Particularly, how comfortable students are with sharing their home and work locations with four types of recipients: close friends and family, friends on SNS, university community and advertisers. Results revealed that both groups are consistently more willing to share location information with close friends and family and the university community than with friends on SNS and advertisers. They did not, however, study how students are comfortable with their revealed information being shared by these four types of recipients. While their findings revealed that both groups share many similarities in information revealing preferences, they differ in the level of personal information to be shared with different groups of people/organizations. For instance, US students were significantly more comfortable about sharing their location at 'work' than their location at 'home'; but Chinese students are being equally concerned in revealing both locations (Lin et al. 2013). Furthermore, Lin et al. (2013) pointed out that the more conservativeness of the East Asian people (particularly Chinese) in information revealing might contribute to these observed differences (Chen 1995, Asai and Barnlund 1998).

3   Our Study

3.1   Study Goal and Motivation

Our study is mainly motivated by the perplexing behavioral paradox the SNSs have brought to (Chinese) college students: on one hand, they claim that they are concerned about online privacy; on the other hand, they seem to be reckless when it is time to configure their privacy settings. Particularly, at the beginning of our research, we outlined the following goals:

(1) How comfortable users are with sharing various types of personal information to five types of recipients: Close Friends and Family, Friends on SNSs, University Community, Advertisers and Complete Strangers? The first four were included in a recent study by Lin et al. (2013), however, the information they studied only include work and home locations.
(2) How comfortable users are with the five types of recipients sharing their personal information?
(3) Does privacy paradox exist among students in an American University located in China?

3.2   Data Collection and Cleaning

Similar to the bulk of previous studies, among them, (Wang et al. 2011; Govani and Pashley 2005; Ur and Wang 2013; Yoo and Huang 2011; Lin et al. 2013; Taddicken 2013), a pilot study was administrated during March to May of 2014 in which a questionnaire is distributed to each undergraduate student enrolled in five classes where the author is the instructor. All participants filled the questionnaire voluntarily either in class or after the class; all have signed an agreement allowing us to analyze the data and publish the words for research purposes. All questions and instructions are written in Chinese (their native language). Students are required not to put their name or identity on the questionnaire (for anonymity). We received 43 answers, in which 1 returned questionnaire contains missing data; among the 43 students, 30 are female, 12 are male.

This study reports 42 valid answers. From here on, we will use subject to refer to students in this paper.

3.3 Study Protocol and Reliability Analysis

We followed the study procedure of earlier works by (Wang et al. 2011; Govani and Pashley 2005; McMahon and Cohen 2009; Ur and Wang 2013; Yoo and Huang 2011; Lin et al. 2013). We first collected demographic information and students' internet-using habits; we then with some questions about students' familiarity about popular social networking sites, attitudes and beliefs towards SNSs in general and QQ (a hugely popular Chinese SNS). Students degree of tendency to share (and be shared) personal information to five groups of recipients: Close Friends and Family (CFF), Friends on SNSs (FSNS), University Community (UC), Complete Strangers (CS) and Advertisers (A).

Before we analyze the data, we tested the inter-item reliability of two groups of items (on user familiarity and beliefs of SNSs respectively) with a total of 93 and 95 content items respectively using Cronbach's alpha (Cronbach 1951). The alpha value shows the extent to which items in the questionnaire measure the same underlying concept; that is, how strongly they correlate with each other. An alpha value above .7 indicated that the contents are considered reliable (Cronbach 1951). The alpha values of the two group items (with 93 and 95 content items) are 0.8827 and 0.9742 respectively which suggests the very high reliability of our data.

4 Results and Discussions

4.1 Familiarity with SNSs and General Statistics

We listed a total of 16 most popular SNSs among young and educated Chinese students, and ask them to indicate their familiarity of them on a 5-point liker scale). In additions to the wildly popular SNSs in the west, some extremely popular Chinese ones are also included, such as QQ, RenRen, WeChat, Weibo, Taobao and Kaixin. Among them, KaiXin and RenRen were also studied in (Wang et al. 2011). A familiarity score for each subject was computed by averaging subjects' answers to these 18 sites. The higher the score, the more familiar the subject is with the site. The result was plotted in Fig. 1. Results shows that the top three most popular SNSs are QQ ($M = 4.8$, $SD = 0.64$), Taobao ($M = 3.96$; $SD = 1.20$) (a popular shopping site) and WeChat ($M = 3.95$; $SD = 1.25$).

None of the subjects use their real name to register in the social network (except for RenRen); only 2 % of the subjects use their own photo as profile photos, while 93 % use friends' photos! When asked how often they change their password, 60 % claim that they never change their password, 24 % change the password once in a year. However, 80 % of the subjects are either concerned or very concerned about their online security. These two conflicting results are in line with previous results that privacy paradox exists (Taddicken 2013; Gross and Acquisti 2005; Thelwall 2008; Lewis et al. 2008; Govani and Pashley 2005). To further examine subjects' privacy

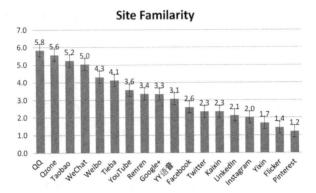

Fig. 1. Site familiarity

awareness, we asked whether they noticed that when they post status through Weibo or RenRen, their address will automatically be shown below their status, a surprising number of 71 % did notice this potential threat, and 74 % expressed deep concern on this phenomena, which shows that the discrepancy between privacy attitudes and behaviors also exist among Chinese users.

4.2   The Visibility Spectrum of Privacy Information Disclosure

Prior studies have recognized the complexity of users' privacy information sharing preferences (Utz and Kramer 2009; Lin et al. 2013), and pointed out that the level of revelation might differ among different types of audiences/recipients. We conducted a more complete study of this issue, and report our findings here.

Students' Willingness to Share Information to Different Types of Audiences. We first investigated students' willingness to self-disclose their personal information to four different types of recipients. Complete strangers group was added in order to establish baseline measurement among the rest of the four groups, as well be compared with Advertisers. Hence, a more complete study was conducted to unfold two key issues that were not well studied in the majority of existing research: (1). whether users are more reluctant to reveal personal information to online strangers, and (2). between strangers and advertisers, whom they trust more?

Figure 2 shows partial and yet interesting results. When it comes to disclosing hobbies/interests, students trust their university community ($M = 4.2$, $SD = 1.2$) more than close friends and families ($M = 4.1$, $SD = 1.1$); between strangers and advertisers, trust is higher in the former ($M = 2.7$, SD = 1.5) than the latter ($M = 1.8$, $SD = 1.3$). Students indicated a higher tendency to disclosure their real name to the university community ($M = 4.1$, $SD = 0.9$) than to close friends/family ($M = 3.9$, $SD = 1.5$). Overall, students allow higher visibility of almost all their personal information to close friends/family than the rest of the four types of audiences, which is in line with previous research (Lin et al. 2013, Utz and Kramer 2009). Surprisingly, students placed

	Personal Information	Types of Audiences									
		Close Friends/Family		University Community		Friends on SNSs		Complete Strangers		Advertisers	
		M	SD	M	SD	M	SD	M	SD	M	SD
	Real name	3.9	1.5	4.1	0.9	2.2	1.3	1.4	0.7	1.4	0.8
	Gender	4.8	0.5	4.4	1.4	4.1	1.1	2.9	1.7	1.9	1.3
Photos	Personal photo(s)	3.6	1.3	3.1	1.3	2.3	1.3	1.4	0.8	1.4	0.9
	Family photo(s)	3.4	1.6	2.6	1.2	2.0	1.2	1.4	0.9	1.2	0.7
	Internet Photos/videos	4.4	0.9	4.1	1.3	4.2	1.1	2.7	1.7	2.0	1.5
	Birthday	4.3	1.2	3.8	1.3	3.1	1.6	2.0	1.5	1.7	1.2
Addresses	Home address	2.8	1.6	2.3	1.3	1.6	1.0	1.2	0.5	1.2	0.5
	School address	3.0	1.6	3.6	1.1	1.9	1.1	1.2	0.6	1.3	0.7
Phone Numbers	Home phone number	2.7	1.5	2.0	1.2	1.5	0.9	1.2	0.5	1.2	0.5
	Cell phone number	3.3	1.5	3.0	1.3	1.7	1.0	1.2	0.5	1.3	0.8
Emails	School email address	4.0	3.6	3.6	1.5	2.4	1.5	1.5	1.0	1.4	0.7
	Private email address (e.g. QQ)	3.5	1.5	3.4	1.1	3.0	5.1	1.6	1.1	1.5	0.9
General interests/hobbies	Hobbies/interests	4.1	1.1	4.2	1.2	3.9	1.2	2.7	1.5	1.8	1.3
	Mood	4.1	1.1	3.8	1.3	3.7	1.2	2.2	1.3	1.8	1.3

Fig. 2. Users' willingness to share some personal information with different types of audiences

Table 1. Average degree of willingness to share personal information to different groups of audiences.

Degree of willingness to share personal information with:	Mean	SD
Close Friends and Family	3.8	0.6
University Community	3.6	0.1
Friends on SNSs	3.0	0.9
Complete Strangers	2.0	0.4
Advertisers	1.6	0.4

higher trust in complete strangers than advertisers, with the overall average ratings of 2.0 ($SD = 0.4$) and 1.6 ($SD = 0.4$) respectively. In other words, they are more willing to share their information with the strangers they met online than advertisers. Table 1 summarizes and compares the overall average ratings.

Students' Willingness to *Be Shared* Information to Different Types of Audiences.
On the other side, when asked the degree of comfort if the same type of information was to be shared by different types of the groups, they showed consistently more reluctance (Fig. 3). Only their gender ($M = 3.8$, $SD = 1.3$), Internet photos/videos ($M = 4.0$, $SD = 1.4$), birthday ($M = 3.3$, $SD = 1.4$), hobbies and interests ($M = 3.7$, $SD = 1.4$), received higher ratings than the rest. Addresses including home ($M = 2.0$, $SD = 1.4$) and school ($M = 2.5$, $SD = 1.5$), emails including school ($M = 2.8$, $SD = 1.5$) and private email address ($M = 2.5$, $SD = 1.5$), personal ($M = 2.5$, $SD = 1.5$) and family photos ($M = 2.5$, $SD = 1.5$) received lower ratings, which indicated that users are very cautious

when such identifiable personal information was revealed. As for the overall average ratings, the order in which students are comfortable with being shared information by the four groups is the same, though the students are more overwhelmingly agree with the sharing (with small standard deviations across all groups). Our study further revealed that, among the four types of recipients, students' are most reluctant to be shared personal information by advertisers ($M = 1.5$, $SD = 0.4$), as low as not sharing at all.

	Personal Information	Types of Data Distributors									
		Close Friends/Family		University Community		Friends on SNSs		Complete Strangers		Advertisers	
		M	SD	M	SD	M	SD	M	SD	M	SD
	Real name	2.7	1.5	2.7	1.3	1.9	1.2	1.4	0.8	1.2	0.6
	Gender	3.8	1.3	3.3	1.4	2.9	1.6	2.1	1.4	1.9	1.4
Photos	Personal photo(s)	2.5	1.5	2.3	1.4	1.8	1.2	1.4	0.8	1.3	0.7
	Family photo(s)	2.5	1.5	2.1	1.3	2.0	1.4	1.4	0.8	1.3	0.8
	Internet Photos/videos	4.0	1.4	3.5	1.5	3.1	1.8	2.3	1.6	1.9	1.5
	Birthday	3.3	1.4	2.9	1.3	2.3	1.6	1.8	1.3	1.5	1.2
Addresses	Home address	2.0	1.4	1.8	1.2	1.8	1.1	1.2	0.6	1.1	0.3
	School address	2.5	1.5	2.5	1.4	1.7	1.0	1.3	0.6	1.1	0.4
Phone Numbers	Home phone number	2.0	1.4	1.8	1.2	1.6	1.1	1.2	0.6	1.1	0.3
	Cell phone number	2.1	1.4	2.3	1.3	1.7	1.2	1.2	0.6	1.1	0.3
Emails	School email address	2.8	1.5	2.9	1.4	2.3	1.5	1.6	1.2	1.3	0.9
	Private email address (e.g. QQ)	2.5	1.5	2.6	1.4	2.1	1.4	1.4	0.9	1.3	0.9
General interests/hobbies	Hobbies/interests	3.7	1.4	3.5	1.4	3.2	1.7	2.2	1.5	1.8	1.4
	Mood	3.3	1.6	3.2	1.5	3.0	1.7	2.0	1.4	1.8	1.4

Fig. 3. Users' willingness *to be shared* some personal information by different types of audiences

Combined these two sides of the analysis, the findings suggest that overall, students feel more comfortable *actively* sharing personal information *with* the types of audiences than *being shared by* these audiences of their personal details. They are more nervous over their information being revealed by others. Figure 4 visually compares the two aspects of sharing.

4.3   Privacy Paradox

In additions to obtaining students' feedbacks on their privacy attitudes in general, we also administered questions on their privacy practices in QQ, the most popular virtual communities in China with more than 815 active user accounts as of December 2014 (Tencent 2015). We focus on results drawn from those questions shown their privacy paradox, and reflecting 43 users. Figure 5 summarizes some key findings.

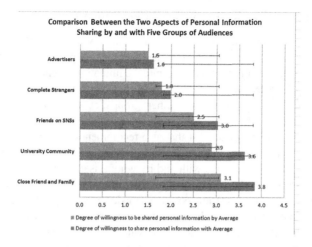

Fig. 4. The visual comparison of the two aspects of sharing.

No. of Friends in QQ	0-100	101-200	201-300	301-500	500+
	14%	18.6%	44..2%	23.3%	0
Accepted a possible stranger's friend request	Yes	No			
	55.8%	44.2%			
No. of time accepted the request	1-5	6-10	11-15	16+	
	65.1%	18.6%	4.7%	11.6%	
Have you modified privacy settings on QQ since creating the account?	Yes	No			
	88.4%	11.6%			
How secure your information is safe in QQ?	14%	69.8%		9.3%	7%
The last time you checked or modified your settings	1 week	1 month	3 months	6 months	6 months+
	7%	27.9%	30.2%	11.6%	23.3%

Fig. 5. The privacy paradox as reflected in some QQ setting.

44.2 % of students indicated that they have more than 200 friends in QQ; more than half of them (55.8 %) admitted that they accepted friend request to complete strangers: among these, 65.1 % added a stranger's request between one to five times. While a majority of almost 70 % has doubt over the security of their privacy information in QQ, almost half of them admitted revisiting or changing the QQ privacy setting only happened in the last 3 or 6 months. The results implied that Chinese young Internet users have difficulties reconciling their desire to be open and reluctance to reveal private information, a phenomenon consistent with previous studies on Western users (Taddicken 2013; Gross and Acquisti 2005; Thelwall 2008; Lewis et al. 2008; Govani and Pashley 2005).

4.4   Design Implications for Recommendation Systems

One of the major contributions of our study is to initially look into two aspects of the personal information disclosure and sharing: the differences of personal information shared by and with different types of audiences. Despite the limitations mentioned in the previous section, our study revealed that among the five types of recipient's, students placed the least trust on *Advertisers*, among four other groups as *Close Friends and Family*, *University Community*, *Friends on the Social Networking Sites*, and *Complete (online) Strangers*. Hence, our findings suggest that as a recommendation service provider, a RS should take extra cautious when obtaining personal information from users and later share the information with the advertisers with and by whom users demonstrated the strongest reluctance to *share* and *be shared* information. Naturally, the more information a RS can obtain, the better a recommendation could be made, especially when these pieces of information are related to users' behavioral data that are otherwise cannot be obtained. Furthermore, such cautious would better be shown with greater transparent privacy policies and privacy controls (Stutzman et al. 2011). Hence, it is important and useful for both designers and policy-makers to be aware of the relationship between privacy attitudes and privacy control practices among Chinese users in social network sites.

5   Concluding Remarks and Future Work

Unlike the majority of previous studies that revealed users' self-disclosure practices and attitudes in SNSs, our study is the first and only an initial investigation into the two aspects of the personal information disclosure and sharing: the differences of personal information shared by and with different types of audiences.

Our study revealed that among the five types of recipient's, students placed the least trust on Advertisers, among four other groups as Close Friends and Family, University Community, Friends on the Social Networking Sites, and Complete (online) Strangers. Overall, students feel more comfortable actively sharing personal information with the types of audiences than being shared by these audiences of their personal details. Additionally, consistent with previous studies, our results found out that privacy paradox also exists among young Chinese users. However, since our study aims at the establishment of the existence of such phenomenon, we can only present our work and conclusions instead of probing into the cultural issues that might contribute to it, especially with respect to the special nature of our students who have been receiving pure American education on Chinese soil. An interesting avenue worthy to be pursued is to probe into the extent of which the recommendation can be made as driven by users' willingness to reveal more private information.

References

Akerlof, G.A.: The market for 'lemons': Quality uncertainty and the market mechanism. Q. J. Econ. **84**(3), 488–500 (1970)

Acquisti, A.: Privacy in electronic commerce and the economics of immediate gratification. In: Proceedings of ACM EC 2004, pp. 21–29. ACM Press (2004)

Acquisti, A., Gross, R.: Imagined communities: awareness, information sharing, and privacy on the facebook. In: Danezis, G., Golle, P. (eds.) PET 2006. LNCS, vol. 4258, pp. 36–58. Springer, Heidelberg (2006)

Acquisti, A., Grossklags, J.: Privacy and rationality in individual decision making. IEEE Secur. Priv. 3(1), 26–33 (2005)

Acquisti, A., Grossklags, J.: What can behavioral economics teach us about privacy? In: Alessandro Acquisti, S.G.C.L., De Capitani di Vimercati, S. (ed.) Digital Privacy: Theory, Technologies and Practices, pp. 363–377 (2007)

Acquisti, A., John, L., Loewenstein, G.: What is privacy worth? Technical Report, CMU (2009)

Asai, A., Barnlund, D.C.: Boundaries of the unconscious, private, and public self in japanese and americans: a cross-cultural comparison. Int. J. Intercultural Relat. 22(4), 431–452 (1998)

Barnes, S.B.: A privacy paradox: Social networking in the United States. First Monday 11 (2006). http://firstmonday.org/ojs/index.php/fm/article/view/1394/1312. Accessed 18 May 2015

Chen, G.-M.: Differences in self-disclosure patterns among Americans Versus Chinese: a comparative study. J. Cross-Cult. Psychol. 26(1), 84–91 (1995)

Cronbach, L.: Coefficient alpha and the internal structure of tests. Psychometrika 16, 297–334 (1951)

Fogel, J., Nehmad, E.: Internet social network communities: Risk taking, trust, and privacy concerns. Comput. Hum. Behav. 25(1), 153–160 (2009)

Govani, T., Pashley, H.: Student awareness of the privacy implications when using Facebook. Carnegie Mellon (2005). http://lorrie.cranor.org/courses/fa05/tubzhlp.pdf. Accessed 18 May 2015

Gross, R., Acquisti A.: Information revelation and privacy in online social networks. In: ACM Workshop on privacy in the Electronic Society, Alexandria, VA, pp. 71–80 (2005)

Lewis, K., Kaufman, J., Christakis, N.: The taste for privacy: An analysis of college student privacy settings in an online social network. J. Comput.-Mediated Commun. 14(1), 79–100 (2008)

Livingstone, S.: Children's privacy online: Experimenting with boundaries within and beyond the family. In: Kraut, R., Brynin, M., Kiesler, S. (eds.) Computers, Phones, and the Internet: Domesticating Information Technology, pp. 128–144. Oxford University Press, Oxford (2006)

Lin, J., Benisch, M., Sadeh, N., Niu, J., Hong, J., Lu, B., Guo, S.: A comparative study of location-sharing privacy preferences in the United States and China. Pers. Ubiquit. Comput. 17(4), 697–711 (2013)

Marwick, A.E., Boyd, D.: I tweet honestly, I tweet passionately: Twitter users, context collapse, and the imagined audience. New Media Soc. 13(1), 114–133 (2011)

McMahon, J.M., Cohen, R.: Lost in cyberspace: Ethical decision making in the online environment. Ethics Inf. Technol. 11(1), 1–17 (2009)

Moll, R., Pieschl, S, Bromme, R.: Competent or clueless? Users' knowledge and misconceptions about their online privacy management. In: Computers in Human Behavior, vol. 41, pp. 212–219 (2014)

Norberg, P.A., Horne, D.R., Horne, D.A.: The privacy paradox: personal information disclosure intentions versus behaviors. J. Consum. Aff. 41(1), 100–126 (2007)

Solove, D.J.: Privacy self-management and the consent dilemma. 126. Harvard Law Review 1880 (2013)

Stein, L., Sinha, N.: New global media and communication policy: the role of the state in twenty-first century. In: Lievrouw, L., Livingstone, S. (eds.) Handbook of New Media: Social Shaping and Consequences of ICTs, pp. 410–431. Sage, London (2002)

Stutzman, F., Capra, R., Thompson, J.: Factors mediating disclosure in social network sites. Comput. Hum. Behav. **27**(1), 590–598 (2011)

Taddicken, M.: The 'privacy paradox' in the social web: the impact of privacy concerns, individual characteristics, and the perceived social relevance on different forms of self-disclosure. J. Comput. Mediated Commun. **19**(2), 248–273 (2014)

Tencent: Investor Relations - Financial Releases (2015). http://tencent.com/en-us/ir/news/2015.shtml. Accessed 18 May 2015

Thelwall, M.: Social networks, gender, and friending: an analysis of myspace member profiles. JASIST **59**, 1321–1330 (2008)

Tufekci, Z.: Can you see me now? Audience and disclosure regulation in online social network sites. Bull. Sci. Technol. Soc. **28**(1), 20–36 (2008)

Ur, B., Wang, Y.: A Cross-cultural framework for protecting user privacy in online social media. In: Proceedings of the WWW 2013, pp. 755–762 (2013)

Utz, S., Kramer, N.: The privacy paradox on social network sites revisited: The role of individual characteristics and group norms. Cyberpsychology: J. Psychosoc. Res. Cyberspace **3**(2), 2 (2009)

Wang, Y., Norice, G., Cranor, L.F.: Who is concerned about what? a study of american, chinese and indian users' privacy concerns on social network sites. In: McCune, J.M., Balacheff, B., Perrig, A., Sadeghi, A.-R., Sasse, A., Beres, Y. (eds.) Trust 2011. LNCS, vol. 6740, pp. 146–153. Springer, Heidelberg (2011)

Wathieu, L., Friedman, A.: An Empirical Approach to Understanding Privacy Valuation. In: Proceedings of the Fourth Workshop on the Economics of Information Security (WEIS 2005) (2005)

Yoo, S.J., Huang, W.-H.D.: Comparison of Web 2.0 technology acceptance level based on cultural differences. ET **14**(4), 241–252 (2011)

Zhao, C., Jiang, G.: Cultural differences on visual self-presentation through social networking site profile images. In: Proceedings of the CHI 2011 (2011)

Author Index

Printed in the United States
By Bookmasters